WEALTHY BY CHOICE

YOUR PERSONAL BLUEPRINT TO MORE MONEY, TIME, FREEDOM, AND PEACE OF MIND

AARON SIM

Lasting Press

ISBN: 978-1-949696-40-0 **(ePub)**

ISBN: 978-1-949696-41-7 **(Paperback)**

Published by:

Lasting Press

615 NW 2nd Ave #915

Canby, OR 97013

Cover and Interior Design by Rory Carruthers Marketing

Book Launch by Rory Carruthers Marketing

www.RoryCarruthers.com

For more information about Aaron Sim or to book him for your next event, speaking engagement, podcast, or media interview, please visit: www.WealthMentors.com

CONTENTS

FOREWORD

For over thirty years, I have dedicated my life to training, presenting, persuading, and selling from platforms with predictive precision. Not only has this helped me generate wealth in my life to care for my loved ones, but I have been able to transfer the culmination of my life's experiences to other people who are looking to monetize their passions.

Why do I share this? Because in my experience, the difference between those who succeed in attaining true wealth and those who fail comes down to two things:

1. Having a proven system based on years of live testing, not just theory.
2. The degree of action they take with specialized knowledge.

Period.

Wealthy By Choice, by Aaron Sim and the *Wealth Mentors* team, embodies the systems, proven strategies, and moves that work through personal trial and execution of expert knowledge they learned from international trainers and speakers.

Having worked with Aaron and his team for over a decade to transform lives throughout Asia, it is inspiring and heartfelt to know that, to date, they have positively impacted over 10,000 of their students' lives worldwide. With this book, they will continue to amplify their impact.

You will be able to uncover your personal passions and strengths, which to date may have been unknown to you. You will be working with decades-worth of specialized knowledge disseminated from world-renowned trainers regarding their vehicles for wealth accumulation. You will discover a holistic approach to wealth creation that you won't find in the traditional education system.

Question is, will you embrace what is available here for your life? Will you take action, persist with patience, and create your own version of a wealthy life? Or will you sadly settle for what most do, remaining pacified in the face of huge opportunity and potential?

You see, what you are holding in your hand right now, this book, could be your passport to the life of your dreams. To have money rolling in and freedom rolling out, that is up to you.

You Are a Culmination of Your Life's Choices

Joel Bauer – America's Top Celebrity Persuasion Expert, Infotainer, and Best-Selling Author of *How to Persuade People Who Don't Want to Be Persuaded*

PREFACE

"Learning is the beginning of wealth.
Learning is the beginning of health.
Learning is the beginning of spirituality.
Searching and learning is where the miracle process all begins."
—Jim Rohn

All of us are unique in our passions, skills, and natural talents. Even more so, we are unique in how we live our day-to-day lives. Working in our jobs, businesses, or carrying out duties in our personal lives means that each person's road map to more money and peace of mind will be different from others. This is the missing link. It is not that the strategies, tactics, and knowledge to accumulate wealth aren't available; it is just that no one has taught you how to customize it to work for your life.

With the internet and ease of access to digital media, you, as a consumer, are flooded with information: some of it useful, some useless, and some is just confusing. The challenge is distinguishing what will actually work for you. That's exactly where this book comes into perfect play. Everything shared in this book has been personally used and validated by myself and the Wealth Mentors team, so you can rest assured that if you absorb and apply these principles, you will get results.

EQUIP YOURSELF WITH ESSENTIAL KNOWLEDGE

Before creating this book, I spent months on end wondering exactly how I was going to put it together in a way that would be most useful for your life, both personally and financially.

Having been on my path to wealth for decades, I always looked at why certain wealth strategies worked for some yet failed for others. Even though there is an abundance of information about wealth building available both online and offline, I still found it strange that some people succeeded and enjoyed what they did, while others who got results were grinding to a halt after experiencing borderline burnout. Something was missing, and I discovered exactly what that was.

What I'm about to share with you is knowledge from little-known sources which contain insights that aren't commonly known to most working professionals or people aspiring for a wealthier life. There is a reality that you need to be aware of: The disparity between rich and poor is significant. The odds of accumulating wealth and living a more stress-free life are against you.

- In a United Nations Human Development (UNHDP) report, Malaysia had the highest income disparity between rich and poor. The UNHDP Report shows that the richest 10% in Malaysia control 38.4% of the economic income as compared to the poorest 10% who control only 1.7%.[1]
- Credit Suisse estimates that Singapore's wealthiest 1% hold nearly a quarter of the country's private household wealth.[2]
- New research by Pew's Economic Mobility Project

PRAISE FOR AARON SIM

"What the team at Wealth Mentors has to share is pivotal for wealth generation. They have managed to discern and present timeless principles and strategies that give you insight into the potential you have to create the life you want. A 'must-read' for those who are confused or disillusioned with where to start."

—Larry Williams
Bestselling Author, Stocks and Futures Trader

"Aaron's book is insightful, simple, and full of practical solutions that work. If you want a stronger sense of clarity, read this book. It will help you dissolve the roadblocks to high achievement!"

—Alex Mandossian
Founder of MarketingOnline.com

"Wisdom and wealth go hand in hand. This book will teach you sound principles and strategies to decide the best way you can accumulate wealth for your life."

—Mirriam McWilliams
American Trading Coach/Trainer, Former Director of US Club

"Love it! This book will give you great insight to align all aspects of your life for true wealth! No B.S. No fad-promo. Simple and sound approaches for success!"

—Skip Archimedes
UK's Top Transformational Coach,
2 x British Gymnastics Champion

"Tangible and principally sound strategies that will help you generate wealth! This book is a guide to discover the right vehicle for you to build wealth, capitalizing on your natural strengths, passions, and personal goals."

—Derek Gehl
Internet Marketing Strategist, Software Developer,
E-commerce Columnist, and Seminar Speaker

(Pew Charitable Trust) finds 70 percent of those who are born in the bottom fifth (US) never climb to even the middle of the economic ladder.[3]

- According to the Congressional Budget Office (US), the top 20 percent get about half the nation's income, compared to the bottom fifth of households that share in 5 percent of all income. The top 10 percent of the population controls about 70 percent of the wealth.[4]

My point is that the odds are against you, and my purpose is to equip you with the knowledge and strategies that will help you combat those odds. Because, face it, if you are an average income earner who grew up with a traditional education, you are going to get traditional results. You are already an underdog.

What I share in this book might at times be challenging to your belief systems and what you think is possible for your life and the world. But by working with out-of-the-ordinary information, you can get out-of-the-ordinary results. Don't leave your wealth to chance; be *Wealthy By Choice.*

There are three core elements of the Wealthy By Choice approach:

1. **Wealthy Your Way** – This is the core philosophy of the book. It helps you beat the odds of accumulating wealth by discovering and detailing your natural strengths, passions, and talents. It shows you which wealth vehicles are best to accelerate your wealth-creating potential. That way, wealth supports the life you want, rather than sacrificing your life in the process.
2. **Sustainable Wealth** – Wealthy By Choice is based on the application of timeless success principles, so that

you can build and sustain your wealth for the long run. The market changes as the world grows and evolves, and so many things that work today might not work in the future. This book focuses on the principles that are unchanging, so you can adapt them, express them, and secure your wealth to be *Wealthy By Choice.*

3. **Leaving a Legacy** – One thing is certain, every successful person who has built true wealth sets out to make a difference in the lives of others, on a family level, community level, national level, or global level. To leave an impact that outlives their lives. Doing so means that not only do you get to enjoy your wealth, but generations following will be able to as well.

WHO THIS BOOK IS FOR

People come to us from all walks of life: IT professionals, engineers, sales and marketing professionals, scientists, business owners, executives, accountants, homemakers, doctors, teachers, pilots, retirees, and aspiring entrepreneurs. We've had single mothers with four children learn how to generate an income working from home so they can stay at home and raise their kids. We've had working fathers create secondary incomes using the spare moments they have between work and bedtime, so they can secure a future where they work less and spend more time with their families. We've even had young professionals earn more money, transition out of their jobs, and become their own boss.

You don't need to take my word for it. Here are some of the happy updates Wealth Mentors has received from clients:

"My account grew by 108%...quite a good achievement for newbies like me. Now I am able to keep my full-time job and have fun in the evening to make more money for my retirement fund."
— Boyd Sheum (Options Trading)

"I've created 15 websites and these websites create $40,000 yearly! I only invest 2-3 hours monthly just to maintain these websites. This has changed my life!"
— Edwin Ong (Internet Marketing)

"This has been a great and amazing experience! I remember when I first got my sales, I was so happy because that showed me that this actually works. It showed me that I can make money online while I am sleeping."
— Cindy Loke (Internet Marketing)

How it shows up in your life may be different. It all depends on what is important to you. However, if other people, who are just like you, can learn the same strategies that you will learn in this book and apply them to get results, you can too.

KEY BENEFITS

Whether you are an investor, potential business partner, business owner, entrepreneur, working professional, student, or stay-at-home mother, some of the benefits you stand to gain include:

- **Achieving Greater Confidence, Clarity, and Power** regarding the gifts, passions, and natural talents you already have to create wealth your way.
- **Experiencing More Energy & Zest** to live life doing what you love.

- **Experiencing More Time-Freedom and Fulfillment** by building wealthy businesses that support philanthropic visions.
- **Establishing More Balance In Your Life** emotionally, physically, and professionally.
- **Earning More Money Working from Home** so you can spend more time with your family and children.
- **Adding 6 to 7-FIGURES to your Bottom Line** and generating more income consistently.
- **Growing Your Networks & Net-Worth** by building a thriving entrepreneurial community.
- **Creating a Driving Purpose** for your life so you can wake up energized and looking forward to the day.
- **Building Long-Lasting Relationships** with those around you, including your friends, family, colleagues, and community.

WHAT MAKES WEALTHY BY CHOICE UNIQUE?

In this book, I provide you with insight to make better decisions for your life. This book is different because it accounts for your individuality by:

- **Helping You Uncover Your Unique Strengths** and sense of purpose, which become the building blocks for wealth. Everyone has a winning game when it comes to wealth, but unless you are clear on that road map, it will likely result in burnout and disappointment. Most people fail because they try to force themselves to do things that don't come naturally to them by imitating or replicating the success someone else has had, without taking into account the fundamental variable—themselves. You are you, Oprah Winfrey is Oprah Winfrey, and

Richard Branson is Richard Branson. You need to discover and define your own path to wealth mastery.

- **Growing You from The Inside and Out** by sharing not only wealth strategies that work for your bank account but the finer aspects of personal development that must be applied in order for you to be able to properly execute the strategies.
- **Transferring the Wealth Philosophy** to you so that one positive shift in one domain of your life impacts all other domains of your life, including your finances, relationships, health, business, and personal purpose. Because without wealth in all areas of your life, you don't have true wealth.
- **Exposing Success Secrets** from internationally renowned thought leaders who walk their talk when it comes to wealth accumulation. Their proof is in the success of their students who come from all walks of life and follow their proven step-by-step systems. Of course, you will be able to identify which paths to wealth accumulation best suit you.

To benefit the most from the *Wealthy By Choice* content, I recommend using the corresponding exercises found in the *Wealth Creation Workbook*. These exercises help you apply what you learn in this book to your personal wealth journey. Go now to www.wealthybychoicebook.com/bonus and download your free PDF copy of the *Wealth Creation Workbook.*

INTRODUCTION

"You cannot open a book without learning something."
— Confucius

I'm so glad you have chosen to embrace the philosophies and strategies I'm sharing with you to be *Wealthy By Choice* and get wealthy your way. In doing so, you have given me the opportunity to make a difference in your life, and for that, I am thankful.

Many mornings, I wake up feeling so blessed because I feel like I have it all in life. I run a successful business in South-East Asia, money is not a problem, my health is intact (people tell me I am looking younger every year!), I have a deep connection with my family (my wife Tracy and daughter Cherie), and I live in an apartment next to one of the most beautiful lakes in Singapore.

Every day, I can take my time to settle into the beauty of this thing called life. Even before I switch on my computer to respond to emails from hundreds of happy customers and great business partners whom I'd just as well call close friends, I simply enjoy the silence.

But it wasn't always that way. I started out in life just like you probably did, doing the best I could with the choices and information I had. I grew up in Malaysia with humble beginnings. After high school, I took the road *less traveled* by passing up a college education in favor of an internship with multinational accounting and consulting organization, Ernst & Young.

After dedicating twenty-three years of service to the corporate world and working with global organizations such as Unisys, I finally got a huge wake-up call at the age of 38.

I was 100% stressed out, working 70-hour weeks, and dealing with high blood pressure. Worse yet, I was spending less and less time with my wife and daughter, even though they were the prime reason I was working so hard. Something was seriously off. I knew that everything I had learned from a traditional job or education was not preparing me to live the life I wanted and on my terms.

I was in the United States on business at the time when I was shocked to see queues of fifty-year-olds just waiting to retire at the US employer HQ. With their shoulders slumped, feet shuffling, and a general look of defeat on their faces, I thought to myself, *"I can't wait that long. I don't want to work in an organization till I retire and then try to claw back whatever health and energy I have left to enjoy life..."*

THERE MUST BE A BETTER WAY!

I was utterly sick of hanging on to the illusion of job security, dealing with the stress of constant organizational cost-cutting activities, and worse yet, lacking the energy and time-freedom to be there for my loving wife and daughter.

So, I took my life into my own hands and decided to live it by design rather than by default. I decided to be *Wealthy By Choice*.

It was time to create a business of my own, on my own

terms. One that was a fuller expression of my highest values and what I truly wanted to contribute to the world.

At the time, I was posted in Australia for a two-year secondment. Determined, I picked up a strong desire to join holistic living and wealth-creation courses so that I could literally buy my time back. Courses ranging from:

- Performance psychology
- Wellness courses
- Options trading
- Property investing
- Internet marketing, and
- Personal leadership

I must have spent at least $100,000 flying all around the world just to attend and learn from these seminars. I've studied over 500 texts and resources on holistic wealth-building and participated in at least fifty live training courses. Some worked well, many didn't. I had to fail forward and persist on this journey.

I realized that the reason most people don't attain wealth is that they don't have access to the right information, and they don't persist long enough to apply the right information to override the odds. Odds that are against them – this is a fact. You have to dig deep and discover what your natural talents (everyone has natural talents) and passions are, to give you your best shot at living the wealthy version of your life that will give you peace of mind.

The result of my persistence? The investment paid itself off in spades. I became Asia's first options trading protégé under the guidance of an internationally renowned expert, Mirriam MacWilliams, and generated an income and investment portfolio that allowed me to leave my 6-figure income job as a finance director.

I'm not saying that to brag. I'm sharing it because I want you to know that your commitment will pay off. I discovered that this vehicle worked well for *me* because I can stick to a regime, am objective, and have a natural affinity for data. For someone else who loves people, variety, and expressing emotion, trading and sitting in front of a computer without person-to-person interaction could feel like torture. But, more on alternatives later.

My point is that deciding to commit is powerful. My decision to commit to creating wealth is still paying off today. Not only do I get the time and resource freedom to work flexible hours and be present for my daughter and wife, but I have managed to create multiple businesses that support people by helping them build holistic lifestyles and accumulate wealth too.

TIMELESS PRINCIPLES GENERATE TIMELESS RESULTS

Today, I am an international entrepreneur, wellness advocate, business consultant (including being a certified public accountant), and wealth mentor with over thirty years of experience supporting the *growth* and *performance* of international corporations, Singaporean entrepreneurs and businesses, international trainers, philanthropic ventures, and investment experts.

All that business success, achievement, and impact I have had came as a result of consistently learning and applying timeless principles. By no means did I sit back in my lounge, theorize, and have things magically appear. Far from it...

What I've accumulated here and over the past thirty years represents practical business and wealth-building experience combined with hundreds of thousands of dollars of my personal investment in training from all over the world, in order to finally arrive where I am today. I have personally tried strategies and systems from dozens of world gurus in order to assemble the ones that actually work. That means I don't share anything that doesn't work. It's this same ethos that guides my business, Wealth Mentors, and in 2012, helped it make the Promising SME 500 list in Singapore.

I am proud to say that Wealth Mentors has served over 15,000 international clients throughout Singapore, Malaysia, the US, Hong Kong, Brunei, and Indonesia, educating them how to take what little money they have to multiply massively with a calculable, predictable, sustainable way to invest online so that people can build wealth in holistic practices to nourish all areas of their lives

The Wealth Mentors team and I help clients earn more money using internationally renowned knowledge from experts covering different domains of wealth: internet business, personal branding, share market trading, influence, health, and performance psychology.

More importantly, our students get results, and that's what matters most to us and what should matter most to you. Our successful students are regular people just like you (and me for that matter), so if you've ever doubted your capacity to achieve wealth in your life, think again; it's much more realistic than you think.

SUCCESS HAPPENS WHEN ALL DOMAINS OF YOUR LIFE WORK IN HARMONY

As Founder and CEO of Wealth Mentors Pte Ltd and Loving Hut Malaysia, one of the largest and fastest-growing family vegan restaurants in the world, I believe that true wealth is a holistic lifestyle, *not* just a number in your bank account.

To say I feel grateful, fulfilled, and inspired would be an understatement. I am, in every sense, truly blessed. Today, Wealth Mentors delivers over 300 trainings per year using internationally renowned expert speakers from all over the world, teaching people how to build their holistic wealth through options trading, internet marketing, business strategy, personal life transformation, and healthy living. We teach timeless strategies and knowledge that will set you up for the long run.

The experience of success, wealth, and fulfillment is a journey. It never ends. It is a state that I and many others must consciously choose and discipline themselves to be in, each and every day. I recommend this approach to you too. Fulfillment is in the moment, so we must fill our moments in life with things that are meaningful to ourselves and the people around us who matter.

After spending more than thirty years embodying specialized wealth knowledge and holistic living practices, my purpose is to spend the rest of my life passing it on to people just like you, so you can prosper in your life too. This is my written legacy, and I hope it helps you nourish your life in all its facets.

Wealthy By Choice will help you better understand some vehicles for wealth accumulation, but more *importantly,* it will give you a strong understanding of which ones would best *suit* you as a unique person, so you can get wealthy your way. Yes, contained in this book is a mass of wealth-building power, but you need to apply it and take the exercises in the *Wealth Creation Workbook* to heart. If you haven't accessed your copy yet, go to www.wealthybychoicebook.com/bonus to download the workbook.

So the question is: will you view this as just another book? Will you waste even more of your precious time? Will you go for an unnecessary coffee, sit on the couch, watch a drama show, and drink beer? Or will you decide today, right here and right now, to make a change? Commit to continue reading this book, day by day, and doing the exercises. Whether it takes weeks, months, or years doesn't matter. What matters is that you make a start.

PART I

THE ESSENCE OF WEALTH

1

WHAT IS WEALTH?

The Wealth Insight Intelligence Center tracks 60,000 millionaires around the world and shares some figures on the average Singapore multimillionaire. The average Singaporean multimillionaire is male, around 66 years old, and married with 3 children.[1] This makes him the oldest in the world in terms of *average* age. The statistic implies that wealth creation is a long-game. Therefore, this book only seeks to teach what is timeless. You are in for the long-game. Not a get rich quick approach. Don't fall for the marketing that promises instant riches or overnight success results. It's no different from falling for the lottery. That mentality won't serve you.

Definition of Wealth

Wealth is the condition of well-being. It is derived from "*weal*," meaning *well-being* in English, and "*th*" meaning *condition*.

WHAT EVERY HARD WORKING PERSON OUGHT TO KNOW ABOUT CREATING WEALTH IN THEIR LIFE

Now, you wouldn't be reading this book unless you wanted to earn more money and accumulate more wealth to serve a purpose. However, as you might have guessed, there is much more to creating personal wealth than meets the eye. It goes beyond just simply earning more money. There are subtle and finer elements at play that determine whether you succeed in building wealth or not. In this book, you will be exposed to those forces that determine your financial destiny.

Whether you consciously know it or not, money itself is quite useless. As an object, money can't even keep you warm at night. You can't eat it. Nor can you converse with it and have an intellectual conversation about the deeper aspects of living as a human being. Money has to serve a purpose for your life and the lives of others. Money as a construct is simply there to provide you choices.

So the bigger context at play when it comes to wealth accumulation is actually about creating the life you want to live. For yourself, your family, and the community; it's about living a life by design. You have to look deeply at what you want in terms of your health, relationships, living space, and personal purpose. You have to look at your life as a whole. It's not just about your finances anymore, though they play a significant part. You have to look at what you want to do with your spare time, assuming you have the wealth to support it. You have to get clear on why you want wealth to start with. Without that clarity, wealth will only remain a possibility for your life, rather than a reality.

Without this strong and clearly defined reason, you will have no desire to take the necessary actions to accumulate wealth. It is your wealth barometer. As you continue to read this book, you will get clearer on your wealth barometer.

You will also be equipped with the necessary tools and

strategies to follow through on your unique path to wealth. One that not only puts more money in your bank account but is tailored to your strengths and passions so that your path to wealth is vastly accelerated and serves the lifestyle you want to live. You want to find your path of least resistance, so you can achieve more with less stress – *wealth your way*. This book goes beyond just teaching you to earn a lot of money, though that will happen. It is about enriching your life as a whole.

WHY DO YOU WANT TO ACCUMULATE WEALTH?

Maybe you would like to accumulate wealth in order to:

- **Gain More Comfort** by getting off the treadmill of life that has you peddling the wheel just to stay on top of base expenses and debt, rent, utility bills, and maxed-out credit cards.
- **Spend More Time** with your children, family, and friends.
- **Leave Your Job and Be Your Own Boss** and live life doing business on your own terms.
- **Take Care of Your Family** financially and secure their future so they have solid financial support as they grow older.
- **Express Your Creativity** whether that is through activities like photography, traveling, cooking, writing, dancing, or even learning a new language.
- **Work Less** as you age more, thus securing your retirement without having to trade your health for wealth.
- **Recession-Proof Your Life** by having money work for you rather than you having to work for it.
- **Enjoy Better Health** so that you can do more with the time you have.

- **Contribute** more resources to be of service to others.

Who knows? Maybe you have other, more specific reasons for which you want wealth. Either way is great because whatever your reason is, it is possible, it is necessary, and it must be clarified.

THE WEALTH PROCESS

There is a process you can follow for wealth creation. I am introducing it now so you can make a mental note of the process as you work through the rest of the book. It is the starting framework for wealth. Just like the post that supports a growing baby tree, the wealth creation process is the same. We set the basic framework from the start so you can familiarize yourself with it, and then we add to it.

Over the course of time, as your wealth builds, as a baby tree grows, the posts can be removed and the tree can self-sustain its growth for the long run by drawing all the sunlight, water, and nutrients it needs to flourish.

But first things first. Here are the steps you will need to take:

1. **Articulate** Why You Want Wealth, What You Want for Your Life, and How Much You Want.
2. **Understand** Where You Are Right Now In Terms of Your Financial Position.
3. **Clarify** Your Values, Natural Strengths, and Skill Sets.
4. **Choose** the Best Wealth Engine to Start With.
5. **Accelerate Wealth Creation** by Executing the Right Strategies.
6. **Sustain** Your Wealth for the Long Run.

Over time, you continually go through the cycle, revising and refining it.

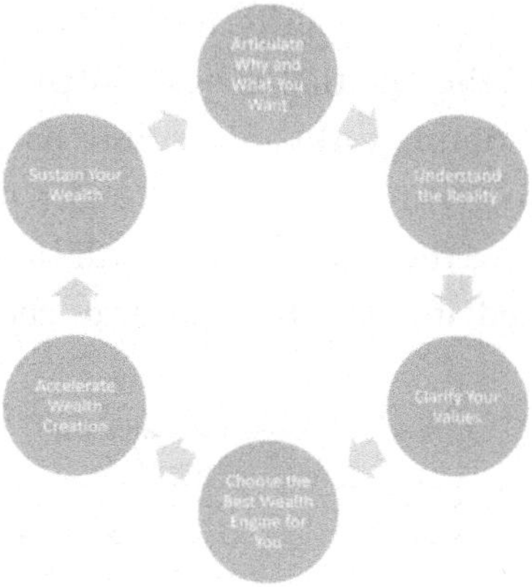

Figure 1 – The Wealth Cycle

I'm giving you these steps now as an overview so you understand the journey you have ahead of you. Throughout this book, I will guide you through the above steps in much more detail and draw on my experience so you can deepen your understanding and application of the wealth creation principles that have worked for me and many others worldwide.

Remember, the information I am sharing has been tested and proven to work, being drawn from internationally renowned gurus and wealth trainers. As such, there are only four wealth vehicles I am discussing in this book because they have proven to deliver consistent results in people's lives for many years:

1. Personal Branding
2. Selling & Persuasion
3. Internet Business
4. Options Trading

All vehicles include timeless principles, which means you can adapt them and continue to use them to create wealth for the long run. The vehicles are different by nature because they are best suited to people of differing natures. So amongst the four, you will find the one that is best suited to your ways. It'll resonate like two tuning forks in absolute harmony. That said, everyone (including you) can, with the gift of their commitment, execute any of them to create wealth in their life. It is not restricted or limited; it is simply a matter of choice.

Wealth Vehicle	Pros	Cons	Key Skill Sets/Attributes Required	Who It Is Best Suited For
Personal Branding	You can earn more money doing what you love - so your vocation feels like a vacation.	Unless you are open to putting yourself out there, it might be extremely stressful.	• Demonstrated value through your personal passions • Sales • Marketing	People who have a passion or hobby that they would love to earn money from, but can't see how yet.
Selling and Persuasion	A powerful skill for life you can use to earn more money and influence people.	It is confronting at first because most people fear selling. But like anything, there is the right way and the wrong way to do it.	• Good communication skills • Great listening skills • Effective interpersonal skills • Able to engage and interact 1:1 and 1: many	People who love negotiatir or making deals, can engage and interact well with others, and who have an interest in human behavior.
Online Business	Low Risk, Low Start-up Cost, Numerous Revenue Streams	Unless you find a niche or have a business idea that the market is really wanting, it can be hard to make it worth your while.	• Understand the psychology of sales • Understand the timeless principles of business and marketing	With such a large variety of revenue streams, the internet can be a place where anyone can find an opportunity to execute success. It is a matter of what vehicles best suit you.
Options Trading	Leverage Time, Low Risk, Low Start-up Cost, High Returns	If you are too emotional and creative in the process – you might find yourself losing more than you gain.	• Patience • Analytical skills • Basic Mathematics • Self-Discipline	People who can make objective and rational decisions, are good with data, can spot trends, and can manage their time well.

In fact, I personally suggest that you get a good feel for all the different wealth vehicles. Understanding the principles to a competent degree will add dimension to your primary wealth creation vehicle.

Everything I discuss from here onward will also be reinforced with personal strategies: strategies that focus on caring for your health, your emotions, and the internal forces that govern performance in your life, ones that you probably won't ever find in traditional education but are necessary if you want results that transcend the standard tradition.

2

WEALTH IS LIKE A LAKE

There is a lake situated about a two-minute walk from my apartment. Each day, I walk through its domain to meditate and recharge or supercharge my energies for the day. Next to the lake is a bench where I sit to reflect on my wealth journey: what is going well, what could be improved, and what could be removed. Not many people come here. I feel it is my sanctuary.

While I do this, I observe the synchronicity of nature and how everything it does is right on time and just what is needed to maintain both harmony and growth.

I was fortunate many years ago to move into an apartment in Kent Ridge Park. Since then, I have been developing the mindset of financial freedom, and I have frequently used this lake to visualize what financial freedom would be like for my life. It has been one of my greatest teachers on wealth creation and, more importantly, sustainable wealth creation. Wealth is a product of having all domains of your life work in harmony.

So, I like to use this lake as an analogy for wealth because if we:

- Keep it bathed in the right amount of sunlight,
- Nourish it with fertile soil, and
- Maintain a clean water supply

Then all sorts of life can thrive. Trees, flowers, fish, insects, microorganisms, and even human beings all have a chance to enjoy the natural surroundings.

For me, the water represents money, which is neither good nor bad, but when it circulates, it can support diverse life forms. Depending on what seeds you plant or what water conditions you have, you can give birth to a diverse range of plants and animals.

YOUR WEALTH LAKE IS UNIQUE TO YOU

Throughout this book I will draw upon this lake metaphor when necessary, so we can really drive home and deepen our understanding of certain principles. To keep it simple, I've summarized this into three fundamental observations I have made about the lake.

1 – Teamwork towards a Higher Purpose

Wealth requires teamwork between different people, talents, and resources under a united purpose, just as a lake survives because the water, rain, sunlight, birds, trees, air, and all the different variables harmonize to sustain it. They all work together to serve a vision or a mission and, in the case of the lake outside my apartment, it is there to serve as a retreat for humans and as a healthy home for wildlife and plant life. Over time, this also draws humans to care for the beauty and respect it. So the cycle of growth and care continues.

Every element in a healthy lake works in harmony, doing what comes to it most naturally. The tree roots naturally find their way to water and nutrients so they can grow towards the sun; the intention inside the seed of each tree is so pure that it knows exactly how to draw to it the perfect resources to serve its purpose. As the trees grow, they provide shade for visitors like me and clean and oxygenate the air so I can experience some calm in my day. Meanwhile, I get to enjoy watching the beautiful butterflies and listening to the peaceful tones of insects.

It truly is a wonder that something can work so synchronously. That's exactly what's possible for you, too, if you work with the resources, people, and elements in your life, and apply them for wealth-building purposes. In our lives when we are trying to build our lake or wealth, it's important to look at all the following as resources (rather than obstacles): problems, debt, challenges, opportunities, and even challenging relationships.

It is then that we are on the path to creating true wealth because resourcefulness is a key component of wealth. The magic happens when you look at the intricacies of how everything in your life right now can be of use, even the things you think are useless; they still teach you something. If we can see how they are all supporting the overall growth of our own wealth lake, rather than fighting it, we can relate to it more usefully. We can work with it instead. We can draw in wealth, almost as easily as breathing.

2 – Flow

The water in a lake is always moving. Even when it looks still, if you look closely and pay attention to the surface, currents of water are moving. This flow is what keeps the water clean.

The water is a symbol of money and demonstrates that it has to flow somewhere and serve a purpose, or else it just accumulates toxins and dirt over time. Respecting this flow in wealth-building means that you need to be clear on why you want to build wealth, and to direct your funds in investments, learning programs, or personal care services that support your objectives rather than simply letting them stagnate. Sure, if they are in your bank account accumulating interest, that's a form of growth too, but only so long as you are looking to put it to use rather than having it sit there and collect dust.

3 – Sustainability

If the lake does not manage to sustain itself, then it is not true wealth. Wealth means that at some point, all the effort you put into wealth-building has taken on a life of its own. In the lake, you can see that the complexity and harmony in play between the different components of the lake become uncontrollable. The trees, water, birds, and other lifeforms all start to interact on their own, as the lake takes on its own beautiful form. It is an eternal journey.

Part of the wealth of the lake is also its aesthetic beauty that you can appreciate. This beauty is what draws humans to want to visit the lake because there is inherent value in observing its presence.

Those who like beautiful things that inspire and touch them emotionally; they will want to preserve the beauty too. They will feel responsible for helping to sustain its vision: to thrive and provide a leisurely space for many years to come and the many people who will visit in the future.

So even when the lake is damaged or falters slightly, humans who pass by the lake are inspired to nourish whatever isn't as beautiful and restore harmony to their own wealth and health.

Wealth Mentors is a wealth vehicle and symbol of this. Today, my team works towards our vision to empower people's financial *destinies* using proven and internationally acclaimed wealth training programs. When I am not physically there in the business because I'm on holiday, for example, the impact we have as a team is further carried on because everyone else understands the purpose we serve, and they bring all their talents and commitments to the table to make that happen.

3

WRONGLY WIRED FOR WEALTH

In this chapter, I'm going to share with you more of my journey to wealth creation and what it was like starting from a relatively conventional professional background. This part of the wealth journey is about the poor wealth wiring that I had, having no exposure to proper specialized knowledge for wealth creation. As you read every word I share, you will understand the poverty mindset which was holding me back, and which might be holding you back too.

WAKING UP

"I'm over it," I tell myself, as I see lines of retirees looking for a payout. There, in front of me, are queues of government workers waiting for their payouts, standing in line with their shoulders slumped and feet shuffling as the line gradually shortens. A general look of defeat is on their faces. "That's not what life is meant to be about," I say.

I was already approaching my forties at the time, and it really made me wonder, *how did I get here, and where did all those years go?* It only seemed like yesterday that I was working as an intern at Ernst & Young, learning the ropes of a professional job that I had thought would give me the security and finances to live the life I truly wanted upon retirement. Years later, I'm a fully-fledged professional, and after spending seven years at a multinational corporation as a qualified Certified Public Accountant (CPA), I thought I had a good life paved out for myself. I thought I had finally found a company that I could work for until I retired.

In fact, the gentleman who hired me was a 60-year old man with greying hair. To my younger self, that was a symbol of job stability. He represented the possibility that I too could secure my retirement. I was wrong.

Here I was in the United States of America on tour for business purposes, representing a prestigious firm, and I felt at a total loss when I saw the many employees waiting to retire. The path I had taken since my late teen years and the traditional jobs I had relied on for decades were not going to give me the satisfaction in life I wanted. At that moment, the meaning of traditional retirement completely transformed. Instead of being able to relax and thrive in my later years, retirement now meant death.

Nothing I had experienced in life or learned from a traditional education system was going to prepare me to deal with the truth that shattered everything I had believed for decades of my life.

How could I have been so blind to see that? In hindsight, I know it's because it's always harder to see it when you're in it.

I was finally sick of hanging on to the illusion of job security and dealing with the stress of constant organizational cost-cutting activities. As a member of the finance department, I was part of the cost center of a firm. During economic downturns or significant drops in market revenue, cost centers were always at risk.

Worse yet, I was lacking the energy and time-freedom to be

there for my loving wife and daughter. Everything I had planned to have happen was actually going in the opposite direction. Even though I was being paid well compared to the average Joe, I wasn't getting any younger, nor was my dream of spending quality time with my family coming true.

Something was off. I knew I had to be Wealthy By Choice, and wealthy my way. Not live by default but by design.

THERE HAS TO BE A BETTER WAY

And I'm going to share that better way with you. Before we embark deeper into that new path, we must understand how the current path was created in your life so that history doesn't repeat itself. How is it that everything I thought would work out from a financial and lifestyle perspective did not work out? How is it that I went through decades of my life not even questioning or knowing that things weren't on the way but off their way?

TRAPPED BY TRADITION

A lot of it comes down to my previous beliefs and misconceptions about what true wealth is, and more importantly, the path to creating true wealth. This might sound familiar to you.

1. Study hard
2. Get top marks in school
3. Study harder
4. Get top marks in university
5. Get a professional job
6. Work harder
7. Get promoted
8. Work even harder

It never ends. If you are like me, having grown up in South-East Asia, you were probably taught to get a solid professional education and work for a reputable firm because they would take care of you for life. I certainly did. From 20 years of age, I pursued the CPA. I worked full-time at a firm and got practical experience while I studied part-time for 7.5 years to pass all my exams after 11 attempts (where if everything worked on schedule it should be 4 years with 3 attempts to pass all exams).

It was the perfect opportunity to learn and earn money in the process. So when I qualified for a CPA in 1986, I got the opportunity to work internationally (in the UK) for Ernst & Young, a multinational corporation with 1000+ employees. I spent two years there specializing in computer auditing. As I reached a senior level and became a supervisor for other qualified staff and trainees, my work hours and responsibilities increased. Ever so gradually, the time I had for myself diminished. But still, I pursued more because of this one belief that many of us hold: you have to work hard in order to earn lots of money.

Now, it's not to say that working hard isn't a good thing. But with this belief about accumulating wealth, you will always be working harder and harder.

Beliefs are a powerful thing. They create the conditions which you have to live within, and at times, that can be limiting and stressful. For example, when people first believed that the world was flat, sailors were limited in their ability to sail past a particular point in fear that they would go over the edge and lose their lives. Of course, today, we know that if you continue in some way or another, you can actually circumnavigate your way back to your point of departure.

Believing you have to work hard to create wealth left me at a dead end. When will we have the time to enjoy our wealth even if we have it? Is it truly wealth at all if you can't enjoy the fruits of your labor?

When following this traditional path, I was working crazy hours for nine months straight just to turn around the figures for another company whose internal audit report showed they lost millions of dollars. I spent so much of my life working harder and harder to help another company reach its goals that when my daughter was born, I didn't even have time to be there for my wife. But if I didn't work so hard, I wouldn't get anywhere in life, right? The belief was that I would be incapable of supporting my family.

CATCH-22

That's the corporate rat race. Every morning, you get up and prepare yourself to go to work: shower, breakfast, get dressed, travel by bus/train or drive your car, work from nine to five, get home to your family and have dinner, watch television or read the paper, then off to bed till the next morning.

I mean no disrespect. As you can see, I have been there myself. It is this exact reason why I can articulate what the rat-race lifestyle is like. The problem is even if you win at the rat race, as I thought I was...I was still living like a rat. You get two to three weeks of paid vacation/sick leave each year and occasional overtime work. You get paid by your employer for your services every payday. If you do not like your job anymore, you will find another employer for better pay. Year in, year out, it's the same routine. You work for somebody else, but not for yourself. You focus your time, energy, and effort on making somebody else richer. This is the corporate race that most of us are stuck in.

As an employee, your income is limited. An average employee earning an average salary, if you do the sums, could hardly put aside a certain amount of money for savings for his/her future use. I found this out the hard way. After paying bills, taxes, my child's education, basic accommodation, and food expenses, you are left with the tiniest of "extras" for future use. Even an above-average employee who could put aside some savings could hardly have enough for retirement use. Let me give you an example: if you could save $20,000 per year, as an employeé, it would take 50 years to get to $1 million. Even saving that much per year is a stretch if all you relied on was a job and savings.

All too often, people become trapped in this race and never bother to look where they are headed. If you're lucky, you'll get a huge wake-up call as I did in my forties.

Today, this is your wake-up call. You don't have to hear it the hard way as I did. You can hear it because you are actively listening. So pay attention. This bit is important.

I discovered that a more useful approach to simply working hard was focusing effort to acquire specialized knowledge to build wealth, rather than being stuck in the same repeating patterns. I found it more useful to follow in the footsteps of other people who have true wealth and the non-conventional approaches to getting it.

People who have actual experiences on a subject are the ones you need to talk to in gathering information. Do not listen to hearsay or to those who neither know nor have any experience on the subject. With wealth, knowing is an asset; not knowing is a liability.

USING THE RIGHT INFORMATION IS WEALTH

If you want to create wealth and be rich, listen to millionaires or people who have amassed the amount of money that you desire, not from your friends who may be as broke as you are. I'll give you an example: Joel Bauer, a world-renowned sales and persuasion guru, did not go through the traditional education system. Joel was born with spinal meningitis. The doctor's diagnosis was that he was going to die. In fact, they told his mother to go home, so she wouldn't have to endure the pain of watching her baby suffer in a hospital incubator.

They left Joel in an incubator (an encasing for premature babies) for two weeks and administered a drug that killed 98.2% of all children who took it. But Joel survived. For the first seven years of his life, he sat in a corner and played with a piece of paper. Most of his mother's friends and family said openly, "He is a retard. He is hopeless." Joel failed first, second, and third grade at school.

Then, at the age of seven, he learned magic and the psychology of influencing people. By the age of 13, he was earning $30,000 a year. By 15 years of age, Joel was performing on Carnival Cruise Lines. He also used the same skills to help huge companies attract customers at some of the world's largest technology trade shows. By the age of 33, with no formal education, he retired and was not dependent on a working income to live the lifestyle he wanted.

So, I wanted to learn from Joel, and other than the fact that he is a great trainer who works alongside my business today, I found Joel fascinating for the new information and experiences he got outside of the traditional 9-5 career and education system. Joel became Wealthy By Choice, and he earned his wealth *his* way. Remember…

OUT OF THE ORDINARY INFORMATION = OUT OF THE ORDINARY RESULTS

Now you might be asking: where will you find the time to learn and do all that? The last thing you want to do when you get home from a long day or week of work is anything that requires mental effort or output of more of your already drained energies. But that's where the solution lies. The solution starts with using the time you have to buy back the time you want.

Once you are caught in this cycle, you are only left with

minor moments to think and act on something different. To do this requires that you gain more energy and vitality so that you can make better use of the time you have and educate yourself on smart strategies that work with the limited time you have so you can buy it back.

Again, defining a "why" for your wealth is important too. You will always find time to do something that is important to you. Think about a mother who is caring for her newborn child; she makes it happen! If it's important to you, that activity will energize and inspire you. You can, bit by bit, with just 30 minutes every day, implement new knowledge and get results. Breaking it down to simpler, manageable chunks will equate to greater progress in the long run.

But the question is how should you break it up? How do you know whether you are on the right track or not? My experience is you do have to work, but you can work smart and with a mentor to accelerate your results. With a proper mentor who has been where you want to go, you can learn and apply their knowledge, gain experience and keep refining. More importantly, they will be able to guide you through the process as you unplug from the traditional programming and learn fresh perspectives to succeed in life. This leads me to the misperceptions that exist around wealth creation and success.

SOME COMMON WEALTH LIMITATIONS

A lot of wealth creation is about debunking myths, beliefs, and limitations that your mind has placed on your life. Though it may not be your fault that they are there (due to traditional education and upbringing), it is your responsibility to change it to have a better financial destiny. Remember, external factors have influenced your position, but if you want to change your financial position, you have to take responsibility.

So let's explore some of the common wealth and money

myths that hold people back. There are many more, but the purpose of this is to introduce you to new ways of thinking so you can start exploring different ways for yourself.

1 – Exchanging Time for Money

The poor always work for money. This wealth limitation means you will only ever be able to earn more money if you exchange your time for it. That means your wealth is capped based on your hourly rate. Of course, you can charge a very high hourly rate and accumulate wealth; however, that is not the most efficient or quickest path to wealth accumulation. And only the very best at what they do can do this.

Rather, the smarter thing to do is to put money to work for you. Rather than exchanging your time for money, every cent you earn can be invested into a business or some other wealth vehicle (which will be covered in more detail later in this book) that leverages your time so you can earn more by doing less.

This could mean leveraging the skills and services of other people so they can help you build your business without you having to spend time doing it, such as in a team business. That means your revenue is multiplied for any given amount of time you invest in providing the service/product.

It could also mean leveraging your time by selling a product to a group of people, such as in stage speaking and training. Rather than having to service one client at a time, you can serve many. People often say, "I'm more comfortable speaking to one client at a time; it's more personal." However, specialized knowledge demonstrates that you can address many people at the same time and still be authentic and engaging. It is simply a question of having access to better training.

It could mean investing in a system that will help you earn more money hands-off. One example is the use of share trading and internet businesses. Once you set the system in place and use technology to automate it, it can continue to earn you money while you sleep!

The objective is to decrease time input for a certain money output. If we take the Lake analogy, rather than having someone work hard and tire themselves out to fetch water from the lake every day, they can simply build a tap from the lake to the village. Now that might take time, but in the long run, everyone benefits. Of course, some controls have to be in place so that water is not wasted and the ecology of the lake is kept in balance. But the tap can only draw on water overflow. That way, not only does the community benefit from the lake's water, but the lake doesn't overflow because the water is being channeled elsewhere for good use.

2 – Poor Relationship with Money

You may have heard before that "money is the root of all evil" or that "money does not make you happy." Remember that these are simply beliefs. If you relate to money as evil or as something that can't make you happy, then why would money want to work with and for you?

Let's consider a relationship. If you wanted to spend more time with your wife or husband, and you secretly thought they were the root of all evil and that they didn't make you happy, you wouldn't be married for very long, would you? If you were afraid of your partner (on a subconscious level), you would want to run away from him or her. If you were afraid that he or she would leave you, you would hold on to them too tightly and miss opportunities to enjoy your time and lifestyle. The same thing happens with money.

If you take care of money, it has a tendency to come back to you and take care of you too. If a person is treated well, they will reciprocate. If you trust money rather than hold on to it too tightly, then you will be open to investing in opportunities to grow your money and leverage your time. If you treat money poorly, then it will return the gesture and become your enemy. Worse yet, if you don't feel comfortable having a lot of money (like a lot of people do), then you will push it away by wasting it away. How often do you hear about lottery winners losing millions of dollars after winning? They simply can't handle the success that comes with money because their relationship with money is one of fear and discomfort rather than joy, support, and ease.

So remember, the relationship you have with money is important if you want to attract wealth into your life. Consider what your attitudes towards money are, then consider what a more useful attitude towards money might be. Then start building that relationship with money because, like any relationship, you have to nurture it over time. You will need to check in with it to effectively take care of it.

MONEY FACILITATES YOUR CHOICES

As we know, money is a neutral and simple representation of choice and a medium for exchange. The choices are not determined by money, but by the users of money – us! So if money goes into the hands of good, it will do good. It only reflects what is in the heart of the user, who then amplifies it. From an exchange perspective, money facilitates multiple parties who perceive to gain more than what they pay for. For example, if I have a program that sells for $2,000 and the perceived value is $10,000, are you willing to invest $2,000? Is this a fair exchange? I hope you say "Yes!"

Let me give you a real-life example: I started Wealth Mentors without much money. I had a credit card charge for $10,000, and to start the business (which involved running workshops and events), I had to rent a business center for $2,000 so that I could secure a lease of a few months. But because I had attended so many seminars and gained firsthand knowledge on how to run events, I put credit on advertising with an interest-free rate of 30-days. I then told the business center owner that I would pay for the room after the event. Because I sold the training programs, I collected the cash upfront. After the first event, I could pay all the bills and reinvest the money to move on to the next event. Like a snowball, it built momentum over time.

Rather than keeping money stuck, I put the money to use and had it circulate in the way I wanted to deliver value to other people wanting to accumulate wealth, and in return, to gain some benefit for providing that value and to continue providing that value. Of course, doing this required that I had a degree of specialized knowledge using business as a wealth vehicle. But the point is to observe the way I relate to money.

Look at the relationship principle again. If you keep your partner stuck in one place rather than allowing him or her to move with something meaningful, they will go crazy and hate you. So why not create a joint purpose for both of you? Calculated choices mean that money can come to support my intention, and we can have a fulfilling partnership that works.

3 – You Need Money to Make Money

We have all heard this before, and while money gives you the opportunity to earn more money, it isn't the only thing you need to make money. In life or business, people will pay you for something of value if you are willing to listen to their problems, identify a solution, and then cater to it. Or, if you need resources to start a business or wealth-building activity, you can always exchange a favor or service to get what you want. It's not money that you need; it is specialized knowledge in the field of fair exchange and resourcefulness.

Often, at Wealth Mentors, many people tell us they want to

sign up for our more in-depth courses which involve an investment that they don't think they have the money for. Whether it is learning to speak and train, build an internet business, or sell like a professional, the opportunity to gain more finances is hindered by this belief that they have to earn more money first. Catch-22 again...

A client of ours wanted to invest in a sales and persuasion training in order to be more effective in generating sales in his business. However, he could only afford a portion of the investment at the time. In his mind, he thought he had to pay the entire fee himself and on the spot. Instead, I offered a creative and credible alternative: "What if you sign up for our affiliate program (ambassador program) where you share the programs we have with a friend who can benefit and you get a percentage commission?" If the commission is 10%, signing up 10 people would allow him to attend a program free of charge. So that's what he did! He signed up for the ambassador program and offset the gap that he could not pay himself.

IT'S ABOUT EXCHANGING VALUE – NOT JUST FUNDS

Another classical example: people think they need a lot of money to be able to invest in stock trading because it is risky and you have to take a loss. However, that is not 100% true. If you learn how to trade virtually at first and consistently demonstrate a stable return, you can reduce the risk you have on your own money. As your skill increases, you can execute a trading plan that prevents you from losing any more than a certain amount. Using this approach, our international trainer Mirriam MacWilliams turned $10K to $2million within two years. She started small and built her way up. If you are curious to find out more, this is something that is covered in greater detail as part of Chapter 9 on Options Trading. Again, it's about applying specialized knowledge rather than having to have money first.

4 – I Can't Increase My Price

All too often, I see people undervaluing their product or service. They don't think they can increase their price. The problem is, without correctly pricing for the value you deliver to your clients, a couple of things happen:

1. You limit the amount of time you have to focus on every single client because you have to serve more clients to achieve the same level of income. This results in a decreased value in your service.
2. When people pay, they pay attention, which means they will take your service more seriously if they have more skin in the game. In a working relationship, that makes your job as a service or product provider easier because your client is committed.

IT IS NOT ABOUT PRICE, IT IS ABOUT VALUE

Price is arbitrary. As long as the value you deliver exceeds the investment, then an exchange can occur. Going back to that example from before, if I have a program that sells for $2,000, and the perceived value is $10,000, then you would be willing to pay the $2,000 for my offer. That's fair exchange. In reality, it is about getting clearer on the value you deliver in the market (if you are going to use business vehicles to achieve wealth).

5 – "I'm Not Good Enough" and Waiting for Things to Be "Perfect"

Many people think they have to have the qualifications or

experience that others have before they make a start on their wealth journey.

- "You know what? I'm not like you."
- "You are a CPA and have a university education, of course, it must be easy for you."
- "I'm too old."

All of which isn't true, of course. As you know, having the professional qualifications and formal university education was the problem to start with. I didn't start to carve out a life by design till I was approaching my forties and faced the reality that everything I did to date was not going to give me the life I wanted: the life by design with my family and for my community.

The truth is, everyone has something that is of value to share. You just have to look at what you have drawn upon in your career or personal life that would be useful to someone else. Did you overcome a serious bout of depression? Don't you think others suffering from depression might find it of value? You don't need a qualification because, by the very act of living as a human being in a challenging world, you have gifts. If you are reading this book, it is likely that you have been resourceful enough to earn the money to: afford internet services, be fed, and have shelter. You aren't perfect, but you are perfect the way you are.

In my experience and the experience of my trainers who speak on stage in front of hundreds of people at one time, it is authenticity that helps you engage a crowd of customers. They are simply telling the truth of who they are, the processes they used to solve a particular life problem, and then offering it in a way that could benefit you.

Skip, our health and performance guru, teaches his ten commandments of health. Before that, he was a full-time gymnast. After years of putting his body under considerable strain, he broke his back and was told he would never walk again. He chose not to believe that and went on a journey of recovery to win the British Gymnastics Championships, twice. Today, he shares his process of mind-body integration so other people can heal their lives and have the energy to create the life they want.

Now, you might not have had such extreme challenges, but you have overcome challenges in your life. You simply need to share the process you used to solve them. With a little bit of specialized training on influence and persuasion, you can earn money by being "perfectly imperfect." As Joel Bauer, our international sales and persuasion guru says, "I'm a progressionist, not a perfectionist."

Using this philosophy, one of Joel Bauer's students, Peng (Malaysian, 28-29 years of age), became the number one seller off-stage by earning more than $1,000,000 in a 90-minute speech. He even outsold his own mentor Joel! Was he perfect? Far from it; he simply shared his story and the challenges he overcame and offered to help others do the same.

When I first wrote *The Secrets to Trading Mastery,* a free gift for our customers that they could use to learn to earn a passive income, it was full of typos. Why? Because we promised to deliver the book before we properly wrote it, but once we made the commitment to our customers, we raced to create the content for the book. It wasn't perfect, but the principles in it were sound and useful. Since then, we have revised the book fourteen times and improved it every time.

Rather than procrastinating and waiting for things to be perfect, we simply made a start – a commitment – and did our very best to fulfill it. The insights were useful for our readers and, because of the value they got, they decided to invest money with us to learn wealth creation. Since then, many have become successful students of our stock trading courses.

PROCRASTINATION IS THE ENEMY OF SUCCESS

The same thing happens with wealth. You might not get it right the first time, and you might

not be wealthy overnight, but if you don't make a start because you are waiting for the stars to align, nothing will ever change. If you do make a start, and bit by bit get better results, then you know that wealth is on its way.

6 – Fearing Competition

People entering business or looking to create wealth think that the market is too competitive. Whether it's an internet business or stock trading, there is the fear that fierce competition limits their chances of succeeding.

Not true. Competition is good. It shows that the business or wealth vehicle you have chosen is working for people. Either there are customers (business) or someone obviously making money (trading). Rather than being the first to go where there is no proven market to benefit from, look for existing markets that provide value that people are looking for. Then seek to differentiate yourself.

COMPETITION PROVES THERE IS A MARKET

Wealth Mentors is a perfect example. When I first went into business in Singapore, I had competitors who were selling training programs there already, and they were doing well. So I realized because my competitors were doing well, I was doing well too because customers always look for an alternative, something to compare against.

Now, our programs are more expensive than our competitors (remember – it's about value not price), so customers are always curious, "Why are yours so expensive?" Of course, we are more than happy to answer that question. We can set our prices higher because we are confident that our programs get results. Every one of our trainers is internationally renowned in their own right and has systems and specialized knowledge that have impacted thousands of lives worldwide. Their testimonials speak for themselves.

"I now have found another alternative for a second income and have more time with my family."
– Syed Omar, a Civil Servant

"Thanks to Smart Traders and Mirriam, I now have a second source of income"
– Wilson Lim, Engineer

"Now I am able to keep my full–time job and have fun in the evening to make more money for my retirement fund"
– Boyd Sheum, Manager

Therefore we are certain that what our customers stand to gain will virtually outweigh the investment in our programs.

We also build a team behind our training so they can provide our students support throughout their wealth journey. That's exactly why we are confident in charging a higher price. We believe in the amount of value we have to offer. So again:

1. Competition proves there is a market, so you don't have to take the risk of trying to sell something people won't want.
2. Competition is an opportunity to differentiate your offer in an already proven market.

7 – The Retirement Trap

Many people who train with us at Wealth Mentors do so because they have been retired for a while, got bored, and are looking to repurpose their life. They tried playing golf for the rest of their life but got bored. So they start learning options trading or some form of business that stimulates their intellect because the natural path for every human being is to grow. Regardless of results, we want to grow.

EITHER YOU GROW OR YOU GO

So it is for this reason that you need to always look forward to something, rather than staying stagnant. Seek out new experiences in life. Don't seek to retire, seek to be inspired. Look again at identifying your Point B in life now. What do you truly want your life to look like?

I needed to create wealth doing business that had a meaning, served the community, and allowed me to spend more time with my family. For that reason, I created Wealth Mentors and have been on a journey to integrate all aspects of my life including my finances, business, relationships, and most importantly, my health. With better health, I can stay on purpose for longer in this life and enjoy a variety of experiences such as travel and physical recreation.

SUMMING IT UP

I'd like you to consider a new way of looking at things. Just assume, whether right or wrong, that wealth and financial success is possible for your life. Assume that anything you think is holding you back from achieving wealth is one of two things:

1. A belief or wealth limitation that you aren't aware of, or

2. A lack of specialized knowledge on how to accumulate wealth.

If you can address these two, then you can start living the life you want and building the wealth you want, your way. The beliefs or wealth limitations you may have imposed on your mind can be revised and resolved using the inner strategies we have included in this book to help wire you for wealth from the inside out.

4

TRANSITIONING INTO WEALTH

Creating wealth doesn't happen overnight. It is a transition. To do this, you must use the spare time you have. You must also address some of the complexities that might come when you are making a change in your life. Just think back to the analogy of the Lake. If you don't have a lake yet and, instead, you are currently surrounded by a junkyard that only has a few useful bits of material, how do you create a lake?

Simple, you look at what material you have now that is useful for creating a lake, and you start clearing out the things that aren't. Then, you put in order the sequence of steps that must occur in order for your lake creation project to occur. It might include clearing the land and putting more fertile soil in place, then planting some trees to first hold the soil in place, before you introduce water flow to the area from the nearest reservoir. Now, I'm not an engineer nor am I an agricultural specialist, but I want to show you the principle behind this by sharing with you my journey to transition after having worked as an employee for over twenty years of my life.

When I decided that I wanted to transition out of a corporate job to start my own business and build wealth for myself, I had no process. I had to figure out the transition process for myself, which included reversing over 23-years of employee-mindset training and finding time outside of a 70-hour work-week to make it happen. When I ran the numbers, I realized that I wasn't going to be able to actually retire until I was too old to even enjoy my money.

This is the struggle that comes with the most common form of income people rely on: earned income. Earned income comes from having a job in a company or in someone else's business. You get paid for your time and services rendered. You end up working just hard enough not to get fired, and you are paid just enough not to quit.

The amount of income you can generate as an employee is limited. There is the possibility that an employee may devote extra effort thinking the employer will pay him/her more, but even then, the amount of income you earn compared to the value you actually deliver is disproportionate – whatever additional profit is gained by the employer as a result of your productivity, is only trickled down to you. Ultimately you will only ever get a small piece of the pie.

By the time you get home after a hard day's work, you are often too tired to focus or think about other options in life. That was my experience anyway. You are, in effect, making someone else rich through your added effort. That's the way life is, when you exchange your time for money unless you are offered a partnership with your employer, where you get a share of the company's profits.

YOU ARE PAID FOR YOUR TIME NOT SO MUCH FOR YOUR VALUE

Now, earned income is generally a safe way to earn money. I'm not saying that you should quit your job immediately. Remember, it is about transition. Since I was stuck in the mindset of exchanging time for money and relying on earned income, my only hope was to create some time in order to acquire specialized knowledge and then gradually buy my freedom back. It took a good four years. Though for you, this time might be shorter.

When I decided to acquire specialized knowledge and make the transition, I learned everything I could about shifting my wealth mindset and the vehicles that would help me get there. Especially how I could put money to work for me.

MORE ENERGY CAN EQUAL MORE TIME

First, I started to get my health intact (both emotional and physical) because I knew that without my health, I wouldn't be able to make use of my time. So, with the help of my teacher, Master Ching Hai, I learned meditation and embraced healthier eating habits which resulted in: more energy, emotional balance, and mental clarity. It also helped me stay connected with my goals.

As I did this, I reduced the number of days I got sick and my performance, both at work and in my personal life, improved. I realized that health directly impacts all areas of your life. Because I invested in it, I had much more energy to invest in exploring the different pathways to wealth in the market.

When I was working in Australia on secondment, I wanted to apply for Permanent Residency, but I failed because I failed the health test due to hypertension (high blood pressure). They told me I needed to get it under control or else they would not accept me. Of course, things worked out in the long run, and I found my calling with Wealth Mentors in Singapore. However, the point is that having good health can be a benefit, and the absence of it, a hindrance.

So with more energy than the average man of my age, I explored vehicles such as the stock market, internet business, network marketing, personal development, and real estate. Any area of building wealth, I went for it. I ended up investing over $100,000 searching for not only the solution that would work but the one that would work for me. I was curious and passionate because, initially, I wanted to make sure I could spend more time with my family and relax and enjoy good health. I was already disappointed at the amount of time I had lost with my daughter Cherie and how I had worked so hard without being able to be there for her critical years. Today, I am making up for lost time! It is also why I have since evolved things further, and now ensure that I also help make a positive difference in the lives of other families too.

The question is, how did I fund all the training programs at that time? Even though I was on a 6-figure salary, the savings I had were limited and wouldn't sustain me for the long run. So I had to get creative with my assets. One asset – a house I owned in Malaysia – I liquidated for a few hundred thousand Ringgit. Originally, it was going to be part of our retirement plan, but after running the numbers, I realized that waiting until retirement was going to leave me too unhappy and ill to be able to enjoy it.

Was it a gamble? Well, you could say so. But in our minds, it was far better to draw on the resources we had at hand, and thus accelerate the wealth creation process. In doing so, I could live a life by design, rather than die a sad life by default later. I was determined to be Wealthy By Choice.

One critical element I discovered was that if I lost the money, I could still recover with time and specialized knowledge. But time lost, I can never regain!

IT'S NOT HOW MANY RESOURCES YOU HAVE, IT IS HOW YOU FOCUS YOUR RESOURCES THAT COUNTS

At the time, I was also working for Unisys in a financial role. I was clear that having a business vehicle was how I wanted to create wealth in the future. So, I decided to learn everything I could from Unisys so that I could keep what worked and ignore what didn't. I started exploring critical business divisions like sales and learning about the sales process. I even got involved in recruitment to understand how to hire and train people to align them for business performance.

I observed the people in the firm who were succeeding and realized that salespeople were not only highly regarded, they were also kept on during economic upturns or downturns. They brought in the revenue which paid for staff salaries. I remember a female colleague who was doing well even though she was ten years younger than me simply because she had effective presentation skills. I determined that if I could learn presentation skills it would be useful for my future ventures. So I took the opportunity to present when she couldn't, and when I did, I felt good. It opened more and more opportunities to present. Since then, I have been able to present and sell useful products and services to people on stage and off-stage. This one skill alone was also the skill that our international persuasion expert Joel Bauer used to retire in his thirties!

The moral of the story is if you are looking to transition from where you are to a position of where you want to be, model the success of those who succeed.

All the skills I got gave me confidence that if I did go out and do business on my own, I'd be able to do it. As my confidence built up and I attended more personal growth and business training seminars, I finally decided to take a step outside the confines of a 9-5 job (well – it was actually more like 9-9!).

ALWAYS FIND A WAY FOR EVERYBODY TO WIN

I told my company that I wanted to leave the firm within six months and transition out of my job while building my own business. Because I came clean and was honest with the direction I wanted to take, the managers and leaders appreciated it. It gave them ample time to prepare for my leaving, and it gave me a good six months to train my assistant to take over my role. She was excited to have the opportunity to grow into a more prestigious position.

At the time, I was afraid. I had thoughts like, *What will happen if my entrepreneurial ventures don't work out after six months to a year?* I needed a Plan B.

I gave myself a deadline: one year to make my business happen. If it didn't work out, I would go back to working as a financial manager or accountant. Of course, I really didn't want to have to return to a full-time job having learned what I learned and being hungry to implement my new knowledge for wealth creation. But understanding that I had a backup plan and that if all else failed, I would still be able to provide proper food, shelter, and education for my family put me at ease. It allowed me to focus on creating wealth without worrying. Then once I was in, I cut all my unnecessary expenses so that I would have higher reserves to continue my wealth-building ventures.

HAVING A PLAN B CAN ALLOW YOU TO FOCUS ON PLAN A

I'll be honest here: when I began the transition, my strategy was not perfect. Far from it. But I knew I had to start somewhere. In the beginning, I did Options Trading to see what results I could get using the processes and systems of US trading millionaire, Mirriam MacWilliams. It worked well, and I got results from as little as 30-minutes of commitment per day (a few thousand dollars per month). I kept my activities consistent and grew my money into something of substance over time. Eventually, I generated an income and investment portfolio that allowed me to leave my six-figure income job as a finance director.

SLOW, STEADY, AND PREDICTABLE RESULTS

The great thing is that trading allows you to minimize your time spent and maximize the amount of money you gain. I would set my trade then go to sleep and let it earn me money while I slept. It is a form of passive income which is generated without the need for you to be physically present. More importantly, it creates leverage for you by making every dollar you invest work for you. I found this vehicle worked well for me.

In the meantime, having entered a different circle of people who were trying to create wealth using alternate vehicles, I noticed that my conversations started to change. We were all learning and talking about opportunities that lie outside the confines of the 9-5. So we masterminded together so that everyone could gain. These were people across different industries, including trading, property, personal development, and internet marketing.

I then realized that trading in the US Stock Market was quite new to the Singaporean and South-East Asian market (this was in 2002/2003), and not many people knew about the market. *No one* was teaching how to trade properly.

Because Mirriam's teaching processes were so simple that anyone could learn and apply them to get results, I proposed an idea to the other members of the mastermind circle. "Hey, why don't we bring Mirriam MacWilliams out and share our trading experience together with others?" My intention was to allow Mirriam to teach her trading secrets to other people so they could get good financial results.

SURROUNDING YOURSELF WITH NEW PEOPLE GIVES YOU ACCESS TO NEW OPPORTUNITIES

They thought it made sense. So in January 2003, I invited Mirriam to come to Singapore to present to my mastermind group. She taught a group of about fifty people, comprising both members of my mastermind group and their trusted friends. After one day of training, they enjoyed what they learned so much that they all signed up for Mirriam's two-day training course, which she ran a few months later.

Students using Mirriam's system got results. Some were supplementing their earned income while others were replacing their full-time incomes and looking forward to securing their retirement. Before we knew it, word of mouth spread, and we sold out another training event consisting of forty people. It seemed that my business was finding its legs! Over time, the idea of having to fall back on Plan B wasn't in my reality anymore. I didn't want to go back to the corporate world. I could see that the success of my business was becoming more and more real by the day.

WHEN YOU DELIVER PROVEN VALUE, THE MARKET SHIFTS ITS ATTENTION TO YOU

At the time, I grew this business with just my wife Tracy. We worked from home and rented a business center office to keep our overhead low. One day, I asked a trading student, "What shall I call this training business?" and his response was "Wealth Mentors." That's what started my whole journey. Did I know I was going to end up being a critical piece in teaching other people how to accumulate wealth? No. Not at all. But in the process of helping others to create wealth, I created wealth for myself and my family.

AS I HELPED MORE PEOPLE GROW THEIR WEALTH, I BECAME WEALTHIER TOO!

Here's the thing: having invested well over $100,000 in many wealth creation training programs, I noticed that many of them only focused on front-end delivery of the information. I knew from experience that the difference between those who got results and those who didn't was consistent support and mentoring. Most trainers and training programs are one-off shows. They overload their audience with content over the course of a few days and then expect their students to implement the new knowledge and support themselves afterward.

I realized it was tough doing it like this and that unless someone is too committed and totally disciplined, it is unlikely they can do it on their own.

So, I decided to do things differently. My company, Wealth Mentors, would provide the ongoing support so critical to success. People need accountability partners because let's face it if you pick up any wealth creation "how-to" book off the shelf, ask yourself, how much of it would you be able to apply immediately? Likely, the answer is less than 5%.

It takes time to implement and make the learnings experiential. So I decided that just like transition, if you break things down into bite-sized chunks, anyone can get steady financial results over time and not become overwhelmed. Remember, it is about giving priority to things that are important to you.

Wealth Mentors is a training business that teaches people how to invest online so that they can build wealth in thirty minutes a day. Our trainer Mirriam delivers the training, and my team and I help provide ongoing support since I was getting results in her system already. Of course, the more I helped others, the more my business grew and the more my trading income grew. As a wise person once said: "When you teach, two people learn."

ALWAYS FIND A WAY TO ADD MORE VALUE

In a short space of time, the testimonials we got from successful students started pouring in, which further amplified the number of customers we drew into the business. As the business grew in 2004 and 2005, I invested even more in learning and attended further training that I liked. These included: internet marketing with Derek Gehl; sales and persuasion with Joel Bauer; health and personal empowerment with Skip; and personal branding from multiple experts around the globe.

I decided that I would apply their training in my own life and get results to validate their teachings before recommending them to our customers. Since then, I have simply repeated the same successful strategy I used with Mirriam and applied it to these other internationally renowned trainers of other disciplines. As a result, I was able to incorporate internet marketing, speaking and selling off-stage, and personal branding into the core discipline of Wealth Mentors.

CONTINUAL LEARNING IS NECESSARY FOR BUILDING WEALTH

The truth is there are many ways to build wealth. For me, it was about offering a number of avenues to my clients so that they have the best chance possible to succeed. That's exactly what this book is about: **giving you *more choices* to get wealthy your way.**

Even today, I continually research and learn about upcoming trainers on the world stage to dissect and stay at the cutting edge of what's available for people to create wealth. As the world changes, many strategies have to be adjusted in order for wealth to sustain. Of course, there are timeless principles that will always be applicable, but technology and trends mean you have to always keep your knowledge base contextual to the market.

I realized that investing or trading online was a very suitable vehicle because it allowed me to learn a simple system with as little as 30 minutes a day and earn a secondary income. Plus, that money can be earned while I sleep. I also understand that this isn't true of everyone. Maybe you want to start elsewhere. Remember, your talents and preferences might lend themselves to different wealth vehicles (other than trading) and those vehicles will be your fastest path to wealth.

YOU HAVE TO DISCOVER WHAT WORKS FOR YOU

Remember, passive income can also be generated from business by leveraging the help of other people and their talents, so you don't have to do everything yourself to earn money. You can have others working for you and then focus on what's most important and productive to you.

The beauty of going into your own business is that you work for yourself, not for someone else. You enrich yourself, not someone else. Your time is disciplined but more flexible because you can make your own schedule. For example, as Wealth Mentors grew and added more and more training programs to its offering, Tracy and I realized we couldn't do it all by ourselves. We needed more trainers and more people to support our administrative activities. So I hired new staff and began training successful students to become trainers and speakers in our programs to help support future students in their wealth endeavors.

Today, this is exactly why I get to work in a business I love and still have time to enjoy mini-holidays with my wife Tracy and take leisurely strolls near my local lake throughout the day to reflect and enjoy my life and business, rather than always being in it.

Because my business requires me to travel and attend seminars worldwide, I get to make a holiday out of building my business. Recently, I traveled to Bali to see one of our current speakers, Jeffrey Slayter, teach people how to bring their global mission to reality by bringing the latest in human potential frameworks and business philosophies from the heart of Silicon Valley (home to some of the largest technology companies in the world). I've even had the opportunity to undertake health retreats and more rigorous health practices. In six months alone, I lost eight kilograms, and my friends are even saying I am reversing the aging process!

Those decisions I made are still paying off. Not only do I get the time and resource freedom to work flexible hours and be present for my daughter and wife, but I have managed to create multiple businesses that support people by helping them build holistic lifestyles and accumulate wealth too.

It is humbling to know that my persistence and work ethic have given me a reputation in the market as being trustworthy, reliable, and effective. I won't recommend anything until I have done my own due diligence and invested in the product with my own money. Many of my international business partners, clients, and professional colleagues describe me by saying, "I can trust him."

MY 7-STEP PROCESS TO TRANSITION OUT OF A JOB

This is the 7-step strategy that I used to transition out of the daily grind and earn more money doing what I love and to spend time with the ones I love most – my wife, my daughter, and my mum. I share this with you, not as a set-in-stone rulebook, but rather, as a guideline because I understand that transitioning from where you are now to where you want to be can be tricky business. So please remember, with a bit of planning and patience, you *can* get there. Like most things in life, it's not always a smooth road, but it's worth it. Remember, be Wealthy By Choice, get wealthy your way.

My 7-Step Process is as follows:

1. **Set a target time frame** for transition. I took four years because I was investing in lots of training before I went into business for myself.
2. **Identify the skill sets and strengths** you already have that have led you to where you are now so that you can leverage these either in your own business or in application towards a wealth vehicle like online trading. Remember, nothing you have done to date is a waste. It is all useful if you know how to apply it.
3. **Identify a backup plan or exit strategy**, just in case things don't work out.
4. **Fund your education** with any other resources that you might be wasting or not using. For me, it was a property I wasn't living in. For you, it might mean eating out less, not buying clothes you may not need or that mobile phone, or even forgoing some holiday travel plans temporarily. Remember, if your "why" is big enough, you can always find a way.
5. **Execute and diversify your knowledge in wealth** by learning different wealth-building strategies, and commit to one or two ways that resonate most with you. For me, this was options trading because I needed something that involved a small time commitment and would earn me money while I slept. Other people learn sales and persuasion so they can earn more money per hour, then buy their time back that way. It's your choice.
6. **Connect and collaborate** with like-minded people who are on the same journey as you, because those who are not are unlikely to be actively supportive in

your ventures. Remember, you can either go against the tide or ride a wave that is going in the direction you are heading.

7. **Always continue to learn** because you either grow or go. The only constant is change, so you have to evolve and change in order to build and sustain your wealth. Even today, I still attend workshops or seminars and continue learning from my own trainers, because every time I go, I learn something new that I can apply.

THE WEALTH CHAIR

At this point, you might start to realize exactly how much more there is to wealth than simply making more money. Wealth is a holistic adjustment to the way you live. You have to look at the bigger context at play when it comes to wealth accumulation. Always remember: it is about creating the lifestyle you want. It is about having a lifestyle by design, not by default.

When looking at my journey to wealth, you could say that wealth is like a 4-legged chair. There are 4-legs which must all be in place and steady in order for the chair to be functional.

1. **Mindset** – Learning and adopting the right money and success thought patterns.
2. **Health** – Taking care of your body so you have more energy and focus to make use of the time you have. Health is about both physical and emotional wellbeing.
3. **Positive Purpose** – Having a clearly defined reason or higher purpose for wealth, such as serving a larger number of people and making a difference. This could be your family, community, country, or even the world; it's your choice.

4. **Right Wealth Vehicle** – There are many paths to wealth. You must pick the one that suits your purpose and your natural strengths, or else it is unlikely you will enjoy the journey and succeed.

Having these four in place is what I believe distinguishes the "Poor Rich" from the "Rich Rich." Let me give you an example: I have learned before from monetarily rich men who are great at generating millions of dollars. They have taught me how to have money work for me, rather than the other way around. For that, I respect their knowledge, as it has become part of my repertoire. However, then I witness in real situations that they are rude in their interactions with others and nasty under stress. On the other hand, they will preach that it is important to be genuine and develop good relationships, and to have a positive purpose, but they don't practice it. They don't walk their talk! Now I'm not saying you shouldn't learn from them, but focus on the useful information. I'm just illustrating what I think is an example of someone who is "Poor Rich."

TRADING HEALTH FOR MONEY IS NOT WEALTH

I have met trainers on the circuit who are hard on their health, "successful" people who look drained and have to force their happiness. So regardless of how much money they make, I simply have to ask myself, *Would I be happy if I had a life similar to his/hers?* The answer is no. They are missing an entire leg on their chair called wealth, and so I would never sit in that chair. I want to enjoy any money I make and watch it mature as it goes on to serve my family, community, and customers.

On the other side of the spectrum, we have people like Larry Williams. He is a trader who turned $10,000 to $1,100,000 in just one year. He works hard but he also keeps himself physically active and healthy by running marathons, playing sports, and taking time for holidays with his wife. Now that might sound normal, but guess what? He is over 70 years old!

Another example of someone I consider "Rich Rich" is Mirriam MacWilliams. Even though she generates plenty of money, she keeps it under wraps. She exercises at 5 am every morning, eats well, scuba dives, and spends quality time with her partner. She is a kind trainer who focuses on what the students need and gets them results. If anyone needs a question answered, she will take the time to answer it. Even if she is busy, she will return later and fulfill her promise.

It is for this exact reason that all the Wealth Mentors trainers are chosen. They embody the principles of holistic wealth and the importance of "walking their talk" in all areas of life.

Even though Joel Bauer is able to retire, he chooses to pass on his knowledge through his events. It's his purpose and legacy. He has invested 5-figures to get a coach to help him get his health together. Since then, his training has gone up to another level because he has more energy to give even greater value to his students.

This is similar to our internet marketing guru Derek Gehl. Derek mountain bikes, spends time with his family, and only works four days a week from home. So when it comes to wealth, I always stress the "why" again. It's not just about making more money, it is about the lifestyle you want to live.

WEALTH IS ABOUT HAVING THE MONEY TO LIVE THE LIFE YOU WANT

If you ever have a chance to attend an event with one of our Wealth Mentors trainers, I highly recommend it. Attend multiple events even. Many of them are free because we want to demonstrate and prove our value to you. We do this to build trust and to give you enough useful information that can be applied immediately to experience results. Of course, at the end, there is the chance to sign up for a paid program, but that's not the sole focus.

This is what I call a risk-free approach to getting results. Rather than signing up for paid programs, come along to our free events so that you can apply the principles you learn and get profitable first. Then you can build from there. After that, you can invest in training and support to accelerate your results. Or as many people have done, you might volunteer or sign up as an affiliate to get a secondary income source to be able to invest in your wealth development. There are so many ways to make it happen!

During my wealth journey, I attended multiple events to gain new knowledge on wealth-building. Over time, I started to put the pieces together. I recommend you do that too. I got to meet like-minded people who became life-long friends. Together, we went on our journey to manifesting a better life. That is what it's about. At the end of the day, we are on this journey of life together. And if you succeed, we succeed.

5

YOUR WEALTH CONTROL CENTER

"Mastering others is strength.
Mastering yourself is true power."
— Lao Tzu

We have already touched briefly on beliefs and how they create your world. In this chapter, we will delve deeper into the context of beliefs and how your mind can either be wired for success or not. I will take you through a process and sequence that will help you identify how to release thought patterns that are keeping you stuck and frustrated and how to install more supportive thought patterns to get real results.

Just imagine what it would be like if you could almost autonomously attract more money, customers, opportunities, and people into your life. I'm not saying that you won't have to do some work. By no means am I saying that you can just sit on the couch and money will drop out of thin air. Remember, I'm about practical and efficient paths to creating wealth with the limited moments and resources you may have. One of the most powerful resources you have is you. So unless I share this with you, I wouldn't be giving you the best opportunity to create and live a life by your design.

YOUR MIND IS YOUR PRIMARY WEALTH ENGINE

Why do high-performing athletes and globally successful entrepreneurs all stress the importance of mindset when it comes to getting results? Because having the right mindset is mission-critical. Recent teachings in the world of positive psychology and the Law of Attraction have delved deeply into many of these areas already. The system and sequence of steps I'm about to share with you will add another dimension to your understanding. It will help you uncover a path of least resistance so you can get the results you want in your life and your finances.

Just like leveraging people and systems so you can earn more money in less time, you are able to leverage the power of your subconscious mind to accelerate the results and wealth-building opportunities that come your way.

"It is your subconscious mind that 'ultimately casts the deciding vote' on how much success, abundance, happiness, health, and freedom you experience in your life."

— Dr. Bruce Lipton, Stanford University Medical Center

As the subconscious mind governs 95-99% of our lives, it becomes a huge resource to delegate tasks in order to build wealth. As Dr. Bruce Lipton says, "When it comes to sheer neurological processing, the subconscious mind is more than a million times more powerful than the conscious mind."[1]

The dark side: it is also the reason why some people fail. There is so much information available on wealth-building strategies, but not everyone is wealthy. Not everyone who reads the material puts it to proper application to get results. I attribute it to one of three things:

1. They don't genuinely want to be wealthy and are only pretending to want wealth.
2. They aren't using the correct wealth vehicle or wealth creation strategy that has been proven to work, and has consistently helped people generate results.
3. They aren't wired internally to build wealth.

Of course, it could be any one or more of the above.

So let us work together to create the subconscious program that works best for the life you want. Remember, the philosophy is to create *wealth your way*. When you are armed with this knowledge, it's like having an employee or system to amplify your workload many times over. This is important. It's one of the key factors that differentiate our training programs at Wealth Mentors. We not only give you the tactics, tools, and strategies to build wealth through different wealth vehicles, but we teach you how to wire yourself for wealth from the inside out and to accelerate the results you get in whatever wealth vehicle you choose.

We complement the mind strategies with the right wealth vehicles so that your dreams can find their feet in reality. Take a beautiful house, for example. It can be large, built of beautiful brick material, and located in one of the finest suburbs of a world-class city. It could even have solid foundations. However, if the soil is not stable and sufficient to support the foundations, it is likely the house will begin to sink into the earth.

Your internal wiring is like your soil. If treated correctly, it can be perfect for growing your seeds of success into manifestations of wealth. Just like the Lake analogy: if the soil is well cared for, rich in nutrients, and mostly absent of toxins, then the trees and other plant-life can flourish.

Of course, strategies are still necessary, especially the ones that get results, but your wiring is a "mission critical" part of the sequence. Before we go any further, here are the steps that will be covered in this chapter and throughout this book as a whole (since everything fits together like a puzzle):

1. **Understand your beliefs**: how they create results and how you can adjust them to wire yourself for success. Remember, many are subconscious, so we have to bring as many of them to conscious awareness as we can in order to work with them and revise them.
2. **Get clear on your gifts and natural strengths**: by knowing what comes most naturally to you, you can align yourself with the right tasks and wealth vehicles, accelerate your success, and enjoy the journey of wealth-building. Remember, your time is valuable and most likely limited. Efficiency and effectiveness are critical components.
3. **Further clarify your purpose** and get specific on what you would like your life to look like. Again, being clear on your "why" and point B allows you to streamline your wealth creation journey and identify those activities that will get you there faster.
4. **Create your symbols of success.** This is a visualization exercise that supplements and amplifies the power of working with your subconscious mind, so you can truly leverage the power of your subconscious mind to identify, attract, and become aware of the opportunities that exist around you. Thus you can achieve your vision much faster.
5. **Generate your wealth affirmations and beliefs.** This is about creating the right affirmations and

beliefs that will support your vision for what you want your dream lifestyle to look like. This is about consolidating your understanding of beliefs and affirmations to support the life you want.

6. **Create and execute a game plan.** This is where you will identify the everyday steps or rituals that will fast-track your results. This step will also become clearer as you learn more about the other wealth vehicles and which vehicle specifically fits into your execution plan.

In fact, I would recommend that even after you review and implement this process and choose your wealth vehicle (by studying Part II of this book), that you then come back to this section to refine and confirm your choice. This book was designed to work for you and with you for the long run. It is my wish that it brings wonders to your life in the coming days, weeks, months, and years. You deserve it because you have made a commitment to yourself despite all the other life challenges and priorities you may have – *Wealthy By Choice.*

How do I know that? Because you're still reading this now and that counts for something. Something very special.

BELIEFS

"It's not the events of our lives that shape us, but our beliefs as to what those events mean."
— Tony Robbins

What are beliefs? By formal definition, beliefs are simply something that people accept as truth or reality with absolute conviction. So much so that they don't even question whether it is true or not; it is just assumed. Beliefs are neither good nor bad; they are neutral. Just like money, it's a matter of what purpose beliefs serve in your life, and in the case of wealth accumulation, it is whether your beliefs are useful for creating the wealth you want.

BELIEFS ARE TRUTHS YOU HOLD DEAR AND WILL DO ALMOST ANYTHING TO PROTECT AND PROVE AS RIGHT

The word "belief" is a Latin-derived term, *"Be Leven,"* which actually means, "to hold dear." Beliefs are precious! So whether you know it consciously or not, you are protecting your beliefs because they are considered valuable.

This is important to understand because things you value, you give a lot of power to. Think how far a mother will go to make sure her child is properly fed and sheltered. Similarly, you can get a sense of how far you would go to protect your beliefs.

People fight over beliefs. That's how powerful they can be. On the plus side, if you develop the right money-making beliefs and habits, then no matter what happens, you'll always be financially fit. Whether you are conscious of it or not, you will fight to make sure you always succeed when it comes to wealth – wealth to last.

So it begs the question: where do we get our beliefs from? Recall the previous chapter on being trapped by tradition. Beliefs are an extension of that concept. They are ingrained in us via our natural environment: our genetics (inherited from our parents), our teachers, our life experiences, our immediate peers, and the community we live in. "To succeed you must work hard" or "you need money to make money" or "money is the root of all evil" are all classical belief systems you may inherit without knowing it.

The process of belief-formation happens at a very young age. There was a point at which you started to give meaning to everything that you perceived (heard, saw, did, felt, or experienced). Depending on what meaning you gave to the situation, a certain belief was born. This belief then governs your actions and response to the situation and, over time, your actions become *habits* or what is known as a *conditioned truth*.

1. You Interpret an Event
2. You Form a Belief Out of that Interpretation
3. Your Actions are Governed by this Belief
4. Over time, Your Actions Become Habits

Those resulting habits determine the consistent results you are now getting in your life. Notice, your interpretation of an event sets off a string of other actions that govern your outcomes.

PROGRESS IS A PRODUCT OF THE WAY YOU PERCEIVE

Need an example? Let's use a generational money-related belief scenario. Suppose John stands at a distance, and as a child, sees a well-dressed male adult wearing a designer suit. From a distance, John also sees that he gets out of a "flashy" Mercedes Benz. Then, as the gentleman approaches his mum and dad, he delivers some news that makes them break down in tears. Witnessing this, John might create the meaning that "men in designer suits who drive flashy cars" are bad people because they made his parents cry. As he grows up, he shapes the belief that rich men are bad people. He goes around finding examples of wealthy people who have done disgusting things and starts to blame it on money and wealth. Fast forward a few years, and he tells himself "to be wealthy, you have to do bad things."

This is just an example of the meaning-making machines that we are and how this can impact our adult beliefs. What are the repercussions? John might take the path of being financially poorer in order to be more noble, because after all, who would want to be labeled a bad person? The problem is, John will spend a lot of his life looking at rich people and only searching for the negatives in their behavior because that's all his belief is conditioned to look for. All just to prove that the belief is right. Over time, the decisions and choices he makes are done at a subconscious level to reinforce that belief.

In the following years, he might separate himself entirely from wealthy people just because he doesn't want to be associated with their "dirt," so to speak. What might this be costing John? What if that belief prevents him from learning credible wealth-creating techniques and strategies from the best? What if it closes him off to opportunities to generate wealth by being around entrepreneurs and philanthropists who are making money and providing good service to the community?

WHAT IF?

Now here's where it gets interesting. What if John found out what really happened with the incident he saw as a boy? What if the male adult in a designer suit and fancy car was courteously telling John's mother and father that a close friend of theirs had just passed away? What if this man, who was the head of a wealthy organization, canceled his critical board meetings to personally drive all the way to the house to tell John's parents in person what had happened? How might things have turned out differently for John if that meaning was made instead?

This is just one fictional example I'm sharing to illustrate the power of one belief and how it might hold people back when it comes to wealth creation. If your beliefs do not support wealth creation, they will continually create barriers and obstacles and distance you from the right people, opportunities, events, and information that could make all the difference.

So here's a wake-up call: if you have tried to accumulate wealth for some time now and aren't yet wealthy or able to make money work for you, then I can guarantee you will have subconscious beliefs that aren't serving wealth-building activities.

Gladly, there is a way we can work with them and revise them. Consider that you might have many beliefs surrounding money, all working together to keep your earning potential capped and successfully sabotaging (with a 100% strike rate) any money-making efforts. Consider for a moment that you may have limiting wealth beliefs. Scary, isn't it? However, now that we know the problem and understand the nature of beliefs, we can adapt and shift them to support our wealth-building goals. We can program your unconscious mind, which is in control of 95% of your activities, to work for wealth accumulation, rather than against.

YOUR NATURAL STRENGTHS AND TALENTS

"Everybody is a genius. But if you judge a fish by its ability to climb a tree, it will live its whole life believing that it is stupid."
Albert Einstein

We are all born great at something. However, the traditional approach to education and working as a professional focus on forcing people to fix their "weaknesses." While this might be good for developing a work ethic and exploring how you can expand your skillset, it means you also take your strengths for granted and have to struggle to perform. The problem is, when you are trying to build wealth using just the spare moments and resources you have, this becomes a recipe for disaster. Basically, you want to learn something that will help you achieve wealth in the least amount of time, so it has to be something you can learn quickly and apply immediately with limited resistance to get results.

By knowing what comes most naturally to you, you can align yourself with the right tasks and wealth vehicles so you can enjoy the journey of wealth-building and at the same time accelerate your path towards wealth with less stress. Remember, your time is valuable and most likely limited. Efficiency and effectiveness are critical components.

Let's take a look at the soil in the Lake analogy again. Some soils and climates within a lake might be better suited to naturally growing roses for example, while others might be perfect for growing lavender. However, if you try to forcefully grow something that doesn't come naturally to the soil, it might never grow. Or if it does, it might struggle to reach its full potential. That's the same thing with wealth building. If you match the right wealth vehicles with your natural gifts and strengths, you will increase the chance of building wealth more quickly.

In this section, I will help you get a sense of what your natural strengths and preferences are so that when you review the different wealth engines, you can choose the one that is most aligned with you.

Below is a summary of some traits that people can exhibit professionally and in their personal lives; and for this, I must credit Victoria Jennings, the founder and CEO of Dynamic Academy and International Partner Solutions (IPS).[2] Using her knowledge, she has managed to precisely identify people's natural talents and how they relate to both wealth creation and business-building. She has over 25 years of experience in the training industry and played a critical role in the transformation of the vocational education paradigm in Australia. Today, she is taking her specialized knowledge to the US and the world at large.

Read the following list and identify the ones that resonate most with you. Especially note the activities listed that energize you and come with ease. Do not simply pick the ones you are trained to be competent in, rather, the ones that you prefer to do because they come with ease and energy.

1. **Generating ideas**, innovation, strategy, creative problem solving, and getting things started
2. **Great at being visionary** and seeing the "big picture"
3. Have a fine balance between working alone, and being around people, and would consider yourself a **balance between introvert and extrovert**
4. **Love to work with specifics and data** and believe that the beauty is in the detail
5. **Prefer to work alone** in a quiet environment
6. **Love to lead a team of people**, even though you don't know how to do the details yourself
7. **Prefer to work with people**, and feel much more comfortable in a team environment
8. **Love to plan towards deadline**, and tick off to-do items every day, and feel uncomfortable if there is nothing to do
9. **Must always be talking or interacting with people,** or else you get bored
10. **Love to look at an existing system or solution**, and find ways to make it better
11. **Don't mind getting up on stage**, and being in front of a crowd
12. **Love to match people** to make business deals, and find yourself being very diplomatic in the process
13. **Love having two phones** and connecting people for the sole purpose of facilitating a business transaction
14. **Good at pattern recognition** and are able to follow a system step-by-step
15. **Prefer harmony in teams** and love to support the team, and make sure everyone's needs are met

16. **Love arriving for appointments early** and would rather have things organized than be improvised

THE FOUR QUADRANTS

If you love people, can you imagine what it would be like if you had to coup yourself up in a room and do something procedural, the same thing day after day, every day? You might be able to force yourself to do it, but chances are, it would be stressful.

Conventional wisdom says that people should work on improving weaknesses. But the problem is conventional wisdom gets conventional results. If you are reading this, we know you want other than ordinary results. Instead of forcing yourself to make money in ways that go against your natural strengths, identify your strengths and use them to your advantage. Below are four quadrants that describe traits that connect with different skill sets. Read over the four quadrants and identify what resonates with you.

Quadrant A – Great at generating ideas, innovation, strategy, creative problem solving, getting things started, visionary thinking, and seeing the "big picture." They sometimes have their "heads in the clouds."

Quadrant B – Love to lead a team of people, always gathering a group together, prefer to be around people, love variety and sometimes are not able to sit still, feel much more comfortable in social settings than being alone, and must always be talking or interacting with people or else they get bored.

Quadrant C – Good at pattern recognition and able to follow a system step-by-step, prefer harmony in teams and love to support the team, and make sure everyone's needs are met, love to plan towards a deadline, and tick off to-do items every day, and feel uncomfortable if there is nothing to do.

Quadrant D – Love to work with specifics and data, believe that the beauty is in the detail, prefer to work alone in a quiet environment, and have little patience for small-talk.

Use this awareness to connect your strengths to your purpose and achieve wealth by choice.

YOUR PURPOSE AND YOUR DREAM LIFE

"All successful people, men and women, are big dreamers. They imagine what their future could be, ideal in every respect, and then they work every day toward their distant vision, that goal or purpose."
— Brian Tracy

Getting clear on why you want wealth and what you would like your life to be like if you attained it is something we need to continually refine. As it has been said, "When the why is strong enough, the how reveals itself." Just like getting clear on your natural strengths will later help you choose the most efficient wealth vehicle, getting clear on your purpose and your highest values in life will help you decide which wealth vehicle(s) are best suited for that.

Suppose you really want to spend more time with your family and be able to travel the world freely with your partner. That means you might want a wealth vehicle that allows you to work from home, such as an internet business or trading. Armed with only a laptop and a secure internet connection, you can build wealth from almost anywhere in the world.

Whereas if your purpose and your highest values are to connect face-to-face with community members, eat out at fine dining places with your networks, and spend time live interacting with others, then you might want to consider personal branding, speaking on stage, and selling.

I value both my purpose to serve others and offer them

opportunities to build wealth, and at the same time, I love to spend time with my wife Tracy and daughter Cherie. To integrate the two together, Tracy, Cherie, and I work together on the business and support each other and then take holidays throughout the year. That way, not only do we get to fulfill our mission to serve others, but we also get to serve each other as a family.

When I first left a job, my purpose was to build a business that would primarily allow me to spend more time with my family. Then along the way, after seeing the impact I could have on other people's lives, I realized I had to expand my purpose. My purpose was to spread knowledge that would raise the quality of people's lives, not just in their finances, but in their health and relationships too. Like the 4-legged chair, I realized that unless I actively promoted wellbeing as part of the wealth plan, nothing else would sustain. Since then, my business has attracted world-class trainers who share the same philosophy. They value their relationships, health, and wealth, and all in their own way, serve a higher purpose.

Joel Bauer realized that all the challenges and life experiences he has had in the industry of sales, persuasion, and marketing were worthy of being passed on. He knew that he was capable of passing on over thirty years of his experience very efficiently in a short space of time. As a result, his students got tangible results quickly. He began to transform people's lives by having them follow a proven system to communicate and influence others in an authentic way. Joel Bauer has expanded his reach globally so that it now includes Australia, Europe, and South-East Asia, UK, and the USA.

AS YOU GROW, YOUR PURPOSE GROWS AND YOUR WEALTH GROWS

What your purpose looks like for you will be unique to you. Over time, it will evolve. It is a question of purpose and your highest values. What's important to you will help you get clearer on what wealth vehicles you will want to use.

How can you get clear on your purpose? A good few questions to ask yourself would be:

- "What did I always dream of becoming as a child?"
- "What would I do even if I didn't get paid to do it?"
- "What difference, specifically, would I like to make in the world?"
- "What excites me most in life?"
- "What might a satisfying week in my life look like – if I could be as selfish as I wanted?"
- "If I knew I couldn't fail – what would I do with my life?"
- "What do I always have time for regardless of how tired I am?"
- "What do I already do that I love, but would like to do more of?"

To help get your brain ticking again, here is a list of things that may be useful when you want to identify what you would like to do with your life:

- Family and children
- Traveling the world
- Cooking and fine dining
- Photography
- Writing
- Dancing

- Sports
- Community and causes
- Cars
- Meditating

Define exactly what you would like your life to be like. The greater the clarity, the more likely the reality. Remember it's what you want, not what you think others would find acceptable.

YOUR SYMBOLS OF SUCCESS

What you visualize, you materialize. This is a visualization exercise that supplements and amplifies the power of working with your subconscious mind, so you can truly leverage the power of your subconscious mind to identify, attract, and become aware of the opportunities that exist around you. It will help you achieve your vision (hence – visualization) much faster.

Athletes, such as tennis players and golfers, use it to refine their technique when striking the ball. They visualize the path of projectile motion so they can identify patterns. In business, you can visualize the perfect sales meeting or how things are going to play out in your business. In the same way, you can use it in your wealth-building activities by identifying and acting upon the patterns that are in sync with your vision of what you want in life. The keyword is vision.

When you visualize, you create mental images on the screen of your mind, which represent neural patterns that help you match up things in the real world and thus help you achieve your vision. I'll give you an example: suppose you play in a football game, and your objective is to score a goal. The written or mathematical goal might be to score three goals. But the visualization of that might be the image of having the soccer ball hit the back of the net between the goal post three times. If you visualize that, then your mind knows exactly what needs to be done to score a goal. It helps you frame exactly what your life would look like if you achieved your goals.

Take our example of the Lake: if you visualize how you want your lake to look and feel, that vision will guide you so you know exactly where to plant things and exactly what resources you wish to come your way that will be of use to build your lake. Almost like creating a map within your mind, you can see the start, the finish, and the pathway that leads there.

Visualization isn't just seeing something. It will boost your results massively if you also add in a feeling or an emotion associated with that goal. The visual symbol or image that you've already created will then start to become an embodiment of all the emotion and feeling behind what you want. Think of this like any well-known brand or logo. When you see Richard Branson's Virgin logo, for example, you might feel a sense of playfulness, fun, or innovation, because that is what his company is known for. Or when you see the Apple logo, you immediately know what it stands for. Symbols are a powerful thing.

When you write down what you want for your life, give it a visual symbol to represent achieving what you want. The benefit of having a visual symbol as its embodiment is that you only have to look at it once to "feel" what it means to you. Rather than read lots of handwritten goals, you can summarize them in a few simple symbols.

I was first introduced to visualization when I was working very hard in my career at Ernst & Young as a Qualified CPA. I wanted more money and less stress at the time, so I practiced visualizing the experience that I wanted. I imagined what it would be like if I earned more money and had more time as if it were happening right now. Out of the blue, I got a new job with a higher income that included great benefits, such as a car.

Later on in my career when I was visiting Sydney with

Tracy, I used to visualize what it would be like to live in Sydney. I thought it was a great city and would often say to Tracy, "Wouldn't it be nice to live in Sydney?" Within two months, I got an offer for a two-year secondment in Sydney! Now you may think that it all sounds a bit "airy-fairy," but ask any great athlete and they will tell you how very effective it is. Having symbols of success helps wire you to materialize them.

Visualization is a well-developed method of performance improvement supported by substantial scientific evidence and used by successful people across a range of fields. According to research using brain imagery, visualization works because neurons in our brains interpret imagery as equivalent to a real-life action.[3] When we visualize an act, the brain tells our neurons to perform the movement. This creates new neural pathways that work together to create memories or learned behaviors. This then primes our body to act in a way consistent with what we imagined. This all happens without actually having to perform the function. Isn't the brain amazing?

CREATING THE NEW YOU – CRAFTING YOUR BELIEFS AND AFFIRMATIONS

"The greatest discovery of my generation is that human beings can alter their lives by altering their attitudes of mind."
— **William James**

Earlier in this chapter, we talked about shifting the beliefs that were holding you back. But what about the beliefs you can now create to actively accelerate the direction you want to take in life? Just like shifting beliefs takes some mental effort to rewire your brain, creating a new set of beliefs takes some mental effort too.

This section, therefore, is simply about creating the right

beliefs to support the vision that you want for your life. It is time to truly wire yourself for wealth from the inside out.

The process is much the same as when you first started forming beliefs. Only this time, we consciously go through the process so that the belief becomes automated.

1. Choose a Belief that You Want to Develop to Support Wealth
2. Find Examples of Everyday Events that Support that Belief
3. Take the Actions that Support the Belief
4. Repeat So that Those Wealth Building Actions Become Habits

From conscious competence to unconscious competence! For example, a useful belief is that "the bills you pay are like your investors." Holding this belief would mean that every time you pay a bill, rather than being grumpy or enraged about paying it, you could pay the bill thankfully because it is investing in your business. When you see them as your investors, you start to look at exactly how much value you gain from paying your bills. From there, new opportunities show up and you can take action on those opportunities.

Let's expand on this example. Suppose you have to pay more for a larger office space. Rather than complaining and shrinking to the circumstance, the action you might take is to sell more products and services so you create the demand for one more staff member, who can then use the additional office space and help you serve more clients. Or, you might find that the additional space can be useful as a video training room, so you can record videos and sell them online for even more revenue.

YOU CAN TURN ANYTHING INTO A RESOURCE

But what beliefs should you choose? Everyone's version of a wealthy lifestyle is different, so everyone needs a slightly different set of beliefs.

The best way to do this is to find someone who is living the life you want, or some aspect of the life you want, then ask yourself:

- "I Wonder What That Person Tells Themselves About the World?"
- "I Wonder What That Person Believes to Have Those Results?"

Suppose you want to earn more money and spend more time with your children. You might then look at Derek Gehl who works from home, has his own family, and mountain bikes to keep himself fit. He also runs a highly successful and lucrative internet business. It's probably fair to say that Derek believes that he can run a big business and spend time with his family: that he doesn't have to choose between them. As a result of this belief, Derek naturally finds a way to do a lot of business from home. He probably tells himself, "I can run a successful business from home." If you looked even more closely at his money beliefs, you could also predict that he tells himself that "with more money, I can support my family and make a difference in my community." Rather than resenting money, he has a positive relationship with it.

Suppose you want to lose weight. You might take a look at our trainer, Skip. Skip transformed his life after having paralyzing injuries. He believes that if you put your mind to it, you can heal yourself. He probably tells himself every day that "I can heal my life" and "I am in control of my destiny." He probably believes that he can do anything as long as he sets his mind to it.

When the statement or belief is about you, it's called an identity.

If you don't want to look to someone else, you could also ask yourself the following question based on what you want in life: what would I have to tell myself about me in order to have those results?

For example, if you decide to use part-time trading to create the wealth you want, you might tell yourself:

- "I am efficient and disciplined"
- "Every day I use my time wisely to build my wealth"
- "As I learn, I earn"
- "I have plenty of energy to make the most of my day"
- "Each and every day, wealth is coming my way"
- "Everything in life is available to me as an opportunity"

The above are affirmations (a specific type of belief that is stated in the present). They capitalize on your subconscious brain's inability to distinguish time. By affirming it as if it is reality right now, your subconscious mind will work with that information right away to help you materialize it.

Now it does take some time, but just like planting a tree, it will grow over time if you habitually feed it water and sunlight. With repetition and care, it will be able to sustain itself for the long run. Just like bamboo, it needs to be planted and watered consistently for about five years before it shoots up to about eighty feet in just one growing season.

Part II of this book will cover the different wealth engines in more detail so you can choose in which area you want to learn specialized knowledge and start implementing the proven strategies and frameworks to start creating wealth in your life today. Or as Joel Bauer would say, "Create a Legacy, Leave a Dynasty."

The Essence of Wealth Action Steps

Now that you've finished Part I of Wealthy By Choice, complete the corresponding exercises found in the *Wealth Creation Workbook*. These exercises help you reflect on your relationship with money, your financial goals, and your natural strengths that will assist you in achieving these goals. Go now to www.wealthybychoicebook.com/bonus and download your free PDF copy of the *Wealth Creation Workbook.*

PART II

THE WEALTH ENGINES

6

PERSONAL BRANDING

"Personal branding is about uncovering who you are and communicating that to the world."
—Jon Low

Can you imagine what it'd be like if you could earn money by simply being yourself? If all you had to do was to communicate who you are and what you have of value as a human being in exchange for a decent amount of income? What if that value is something you already have, but just can't see, and when you do, it could mean a wealth of income for you?

WHAT IF YOU COULD MONETIZE WHO YOU ARE?

If that is a concept that you resonate with, then personal branding is something you simply must consider as a wealth vehicle. Don't worry about how yet. We'll get to that. First, I want to take you through things step-by-step so you understand personal branding properly, and then you can choose whether it is something you want to get engaged in.

"Choose a job you love, and you will never have to work a day in your life."
— Confucius

Here's the thing: often when you ask people about what they do, they talk about their career life. Little do they respond about what they do with family, friends, and their more inspiring hobbies, which is, let's face it, a huge part of what life is about.

It's almost as if we have all been conditioned to segment our lives into two parts: work and life. But is this the best and only way?

The reality is: our work is a means to the lifestyle we want to live. We have all heard of the term "Work-Life Balance." Within this commonly used concept, the two domains are assumed to be *separate*.

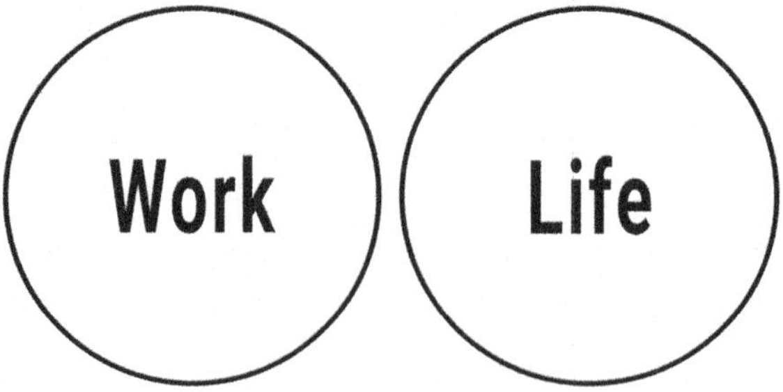

This separation can be true and valid in many cases. But, it is not exactly useful if you are trying to live a life by being who you are and monetizing your gifts, or by expressing and communicating your uniqueness in a way that someone would pay.

The problem with the above model is that the more you work to fund your lifestyle, the amount of time you have to enjoy your lifestyle reduces because you are trading your lifestyle for money. This also works in reverse: when you spend more time on lifestyle, traveling the world, playing with the kids, dining at exotic places, and enjoying recreation, the amount of funds you earn from working can suffer.

A BATTLE BETWEEN WORK AND LIFESTYLE: TIME AND MONEY

Of course, other wealth engines might help you leverage your time and have your money work for you, but they might not be aligned to your natural strengths or interests.

With personal branding, you live your life doing something you love, not simply the things you feel obligated to do. Suppose you love to cook and take care of your children. Then you could potentially start a business that teaches parents how to cook nutritious food for their children! You can do that using your own personality, experiences, and insights in a way that is memorable. What if your tips and wisdom could help others express their culinary passions while feeding their children in a way that truly nourishes them?

In other words, with personal branding, you aim to have work and lifestyle overlap as much as possible. When this happens, you no longer need to worry about work-life balance, because you're now aspiring toward work-life integration, where there is no distinction between work and play.

BREAKING DOWN THE BARRIERS BETWEEN WORK AND PLAY!

Everyone, including you, has a gift and a passion for something in life. Everyone has something valuable to share. You are a human being surviving in a pretty difficult world. The challenges and obstacles you have overcome have allowed you to be fed, sheltered, and educated enough to read this book. Likely, you have access to the internet and live way above the world's poverty line. That has to count for something. You have been resourceful in your own way, and that is a resource that others would pay for if you can help solve their problems too.

SELLING POINT – SAVING LIVES, LITERALLY!

We once had a gentleman attend a Passion2Profit course with our internationally renowned trainer, Joel Bauer. When Joel asked him, "So what experience do you have to share?" his direct and honest response was, "I've attempted suicide twice." He survived both times even though he had tried both slitting his wrists and drinking poison.

As a result of these near misses, he found a new purpose (or else why else would he have attended Joel's course?!). He realized that if he wasn't even able to end his own life, he must have a larger purpose here on Earth. So after attending Passion2Profit, he decided he would start a practice and help other people who have suicidal tendencies. He would inspire them from his own experiences to create a new purpose for their lives.

SELLING POINT – ADVENTURE AND EXCITEMENT

I'll give you another example, a brighter one this time. We had a lady come to Joel's training who worked in administration. She was bored to tears; the job wasn't giving her the money she wanted, and in her spare time, she loved nothing more than going skydiving and seeking out other adventures. The adrenaline rush of taking part in such risky outdoor activities was her passion. So she asked the room, "How many of you would attend a 2 or 3-day adventure retreat doing activities such as skydiving, jungle trekking, camping, and generally having lots of fun?" 70% of the room said, "Yes!"

The amazing thing about personal branding is: when you look deeper, understand the gifts you bring to the table, and create a process and system for communicating and selling those gifts in terms of what other people need, the sky's the limit.

EVEN THE PRINCE TRADED HIS PLACE WITH THE PAUPER

I have witnessed some pretty amazing things, but am still continuously surprised by the number of lives that our trainer, Joel Bauer, has transformed: people who had lost hope, wanted to take their own lives, or had been deeply depressed for years. No one knew, but when they found their passion and saw that their tragedies were resources and opportunities to make a difference and create wealth, they discovered a new purpose for life. They now have hope to live on through their life and be able to help other people too.

"Joel Bauer has brought the art and science of persuasion to a whole new level."
— Tony Robbins

SUMMARY OF KEY BENEFITS

- Earn more money by being yourself
- Dissolve the barriers between work and play, so you can do what you love and love what you do!
- Unique positioning in the market (if done properly), because you as a person are unique!

WHO IS IT BEST SUITED FOR?

Anyone can do personal branding if they have the desire. However, it is perfect for people who are already happy to have their identity known to the public or are willing to move through the resistance that comes with being known publicly. Likely, this means you lean more towards *Quadrants A* and *B* or have a significant tendency in these quadrants.

Characteristics such as:

- Great at generating ideas.
- Naturally a knack for visionary thinking and seeing the "big picture."
- Love to lead people.
- Feel much more comfortable in social settings.
- Find that your creativity and learning ability is stimulated through social interaction.

- Prefer to be around people than be alone in private.

If you are building a personal brand, your identity is going to be "out there," and you will have to be comfortable with that or *get* comfortable with that. It's important to note, it is useful to spend a lot of time and effort getting clear on your natural strengths, passions, and purpose before pursuing this wealth vehicle. If you haven't done so, do so now. By doing that, you will be clearer on who you are and the value you bring to the market if you choose Personal Branding as a vehicle for wealth.

IT'S ABOUT COMMUNICATING WHO YOU ARE

That starts with getting very clear on who you are. Think about Oprah Winfrey and Richard Branson. Their personal brands are thriving. They are paid to guest-talk at events worldwide because of the unique value they bring. They both have their own stories of trials and triumphs. But note, do not compare yourself to how they are now. They didn't start that way. They started by sharing whatever gifts they had in the most authentic ways they could.

Richard Branson has a childlike curiosity and willingness to try anything. As a result, his brand, Virgin, is bold and fun. For Oprah Winfrey, her knowledge and personality are an inspiration to women to transcend their life circumstances and become somebody. As a result, she has built a huge and trusted following. Her books, live shows, and events sell like crazy. Both Richard Branson and Oprah Winfrey absolutely love what they do. Even as they age, they continue doing what they love because it's who they are. They are living and thriving by monetizing who they are. If you have time, it's a great idea to research their lives because as you can see, they are people just like you, and they had to start somewhere. If any of their stories resonate, you can model their success strategies too.

SOME IMPORTANT SKILLS YOU WILL NEED

1 – Understand How to Sell

At a fundamental level, you are selling who you are. As such, it is important to learn the basics of sales, influence, and persuasion. Please understand: this is not about being manipulative. As you can probably tell, my business (and life, for that matter) is all about integrity.

Mastering the skills of sales, influence, and persuasion ensures that you can understand human behavior and effectively communicate what you have to offer. This allows you to move past people's pre-programmed levels of distrust and hate because there are people out there who rip others off and waste their time. However, you are not one of those people, which means you need a simple way to connect with your audience to take them past their concerns and position yourself as the only logical choice for the solution they want in their lives. Because you can help them. For the fundamentals of these skills, I suggest you read the next chapter on the art of selling and persuasion. Trust me, it is priceless.

2 – Understand Online Business

I also highly suggest that you learn the basics of online business because, in this day and age, getting your brand out there can be done cost-effectively and quickly using the internet. Again, it is about acquiring specialized knowledge on how to do that.

For this, I recommend reading Chapter 8, so you can gain an idea of how the online business world works. Not that you have to and want to do online business yourself. You could actually delegate that to someone else to leverage your time, but having a core and clear understanding of the online business landscape will be invaluable.

THE PERSONAL BRANDING PROCESS

Like everything, there is a step-by-step formula for Personal Branding and prospering from being who you are. The following process is something I have distilled and simplified to get you started. It is also a summary of our more extensive 2-day training program, *Passion2Profit*, offered by Joel Bauer. The process for personal branding is as simple as 3-steps:

1. **Uncover who you are** in terms of your passion, strengths, and experiences.
2. **Identify the key needs** or struggles that your potential clients are going through.
3. **Communicate the value** you deliver and the credibility you have to resolve their struggles.

In the following section, I will cover this 3-step process in more depth. You can use it immediately to get a sense of how you might earn money through personal branding. By the end of this chapter, you will get clear on the value you bring to the market and who exactly will find it valuable.

1 – Uncovering Your Passion, Strengths, and Experiences

This has already been covered, but I want to go over it again in a slightly different way that might add dimension to your understanding of your passion, strengths, and experiences.

We live in a society where people share very different passions and value systems. Every country, community, culture, city, and family values something different. The beauty of this is, therefore, everyone has a unique value to offer. This natural diversity allows for the exchange of goods to occur because if everyone was a baker (for example), not much trade would happen. Because we have bakers, writers, restaurant owners, fashion designers, etc., trade can occur.

Let me give you some examples of things people might value:

- Business/Career
- Money-making
- Family and kids
- Fashion and beauty
- Relationships/Partnerships
- Networking
- Sports activities
- Travel adventure
- Research and writing
- Learning languages

Your highest values will be a *determining* factor to help you get clear on what your passion and strengths are.

YOUR PASSION AND STRENGTHS ARE A RESULT OF YOUR HIGHEST VALUES

Remember the example I used before in which a mother who loves her children and also has a passion for healthful cooking has clearly placed a high value on motherhood and health? By integrating them together, she has found a passion and a niche that inspires her: teaching other mothers how to cook and care for their children. As a result, it is likely she is good at what she does because it inspires her. If she looks back at her life, she'll probably notice she has had a lot of experience taking care of her own health and possibly that of others too.

Let me give you another example. If you place a high value on travel adventures and love photography, you could get paid as an independent contractor to go about the world capturing adventure moments. The first step then is to get clear on your values. Remember, everyone, including you, has a gift and a passion for something in life and everyone has something valuable to share.

I'll repeat something I said earlier because it's worthwhile to keep this in mind should you ever begin to doubt your abilities: the challenges and obstacles you have overcome have allowed you to be fed, sheltered, and educated enough to read this book. Likely, you have access to the internet and live way above the world's poverty line. That has to count for something. You have been resourceful in your own way, and that is a resource that others would pay for if you can help solve their problems too.

2 – Identify the Key Needs

What do your potential clients really need? Unless you understand and can connect to the needs and struggles of your potential clients, you can't sell them what you have to offer. Most people are busy, skeptical, and thoroughly engaged with their own problems in life, so you have to meet them where they are at and then take them where they want to be.

Is it emotional freedom that they want? Do they want more time with their families? Do they have all the money in the world yet still feel unfulfilled? Are they struggling with bouts of depression and anxiety? Do they feel alone and desperate in a world that just seems unjust?

To answer these questions, you have to get into the minds of your target audience. Understand their lives on a deep level. Just like anyone you really care for, you have to ask, inquire and observe. When you understand your potential clients, they have the opportunity to feel understood. If they feel understood, they are going to trust you more. People do business with people they trust.

. . .

3 – Communicating the Benefits

People don't buy for the sake of owning a certain product or service. Rather, they buy because of the benefits they will receive as a result of owning that product or service.

The example that has traditionally been used to illustrate this point is this: that in the space of one year, a quarter of a million quarter-inch drills were sold, and not one person that bought a drill wanted a quarter-inch drill. Instead, they bought the drills because they wanted the benefits the drill could provide – a quarter-inch hole. Therefore, talk in terms of specific benefits, and how those benefits apply directly to the particular prospect in front of you at the time. So to sell a drill, you will tell them: "make clean-cut holes in your wall in a matter of seconds". This is more likely to sell them on what you want.

In terms of personal branding, let's go back to the mother that makes food while caring for her child. The benefits she might communicate are:

- Nutritious meals that will care for your child, and he/she will keep asking for more
- How to cook a first-class family meal fast and affordably

The first benefit talks about the care for a child and implies the taste benefit. The second benefit talks about how to quickly assemble a luxurious meal, even if you have little time on your hands.

If you just sold the product – recipes – then you don't speak to the reasons parents want to feed their children. If you try to sell people for any reason other than their own, you run the risk of turning them off or otherwise alienating them, which usually ends up destroying the sale you are trying to make, as well as any future sales.

Make that personal connection between your brand and your customer. Your personal experiences will help you identify exactly what your customer really wants. You then share your solutions through your personal brand.

7

SMARTER SELLING

"Salesmanship is limitless. Our very living is selling. We are all salespeople."
—James Cash Penny

Can you imagine what it would be like if you had something of unquestionable value that could make a huge impact on people's lives, yet no one was buying it? Can you imagine what it would be like if you just knew you could solve some critical problems or meet the needs of the market while making a huge profit at the same time, yet still no one would buy what you have to offer?

It all comes down to one word - selling. Or shall I say - incorrect selling. You see, people want to buy solutions to their problems. People want to invest their money wisely. It is just that no one is properly selling, so it turns into a "turn off." Worse yet, they are labeled as "salesy" people.

Turns out, there is a huge opportunity if you learn how to sell properly. It's the one thing that most people in business fear to do and that the mainstream has ostracized. Remember, if you want results in life, you have to go against the grain. Most of the mainstream doesn't learn how to properly sell. For that reason, most people fail to accumulate wealth.

It's surprising how little most people know about smarter selling. Selling is a critical skill if you want to accumulate wealth through the exchange of a product or service. Anything that requires influencing another person to go forward with a potentially profitable deal will involve selling.

Sadly, selling is something most people don't want to be associated with. Once selling is mentioned, people tend to immediately imagine a picture of a sleazy salesperson forcing them to buy something they don't want, which is repulsive. For those thinking they ought to learn sales, they think they have to go door-knocking and experience rejection before they experience success. Both assumptions are false.

SMARTER SELLING IS ABOUT UNDERSTANDING AND RESPECTING A NEED AND CATERING TO IT PROFESSIONALLY

I'm not saying you can't accumulate wealth without selling, because you can always use a wealth vehicle such as trading to do that; but either way, the psychology and principle of sales is priceless. Most people don't know that selling is part of life. We all do it every day: consciously or not. Selling is a critical skill for life.

We sell our friends on trying out a product that has benefited us; we sell our more attractive qualities to a potential partner in our lives; when we dress for the day, we sell an image of how we want others to perceive us; when we show up for a job interview, we are selling ourselves to a future employer; even the homeless man on the street is selling his dress and actions in a way that stimulates empathy from us and draws on the emotion of guilt so that we will give him money. If he begged while wearing a Rolex watch and a suit, it wouldn't work as well.

Please understand, I'm not saying that all selling is ethical, but my point is that selling is a part of life. We all do it whether we like it or not.

SELLING IS ABOUT IDENTIFYING AN AUTHENTIC MATCH WHERE BOTH PARTIES STAND TO GAIN

Today, many of the businesses and individuals who train with us at Wealth Mentors have a business relationship with us because they were referred by past students who have already had success. If you learn how to sell properly, by understanding the deeper needs of another person and offering them the right solution, not only do you impact your wallet, you also positively impact their lives. What I'm teaching you here is much more than some wealth tactic. It is empowering you with a communication skill that will allow you to build *wealth your way* and live a life by your choice.

Can you imagine what it would be like if you could easily and quickly get to the heart of the needs of people, and in exchange for helping them, earn a lot of money in the process? Not only will your wallet feel good, but you will also feel good about yourself too. That's ethical selling. That's also smarter selling, something that is core to my wealth philosophy.

IT'S ABOUT SMARTER SELLING RATHER THAN BEING "SALESY"

In this chapter, I am going to cover why selling is important, who it is best suited to, and some useful selling tips you can use to enhance the way you interact with people daily. It will expand your ability to influence others to get what you want in a way that they get what they want too.

WHY SELL?

If you are in business for yourself, or carry out money-making activities that require interaction with people or potential clients, you owe it to them to be as effective a salesperson as you can be. By doing that, you'll end up advising them on better solutions to serve their needs. This saves them both time and money and helps them to have greater peace of mind on the decision they have made in buying from you. They will feel good about their choice, likely get results, and then come back to you for more. Either that or they will refer more customers to you.

SELLING ALLOWS YOU TO POSITIVELY IMPACT PEOPLE'S LIVES

If you are in the workplace, selling also helps you get what you want, whether that is in negotiating your position on a project you want to work on or negotiating a salary. You will learn how to get into other people's worlds and understand what they need so that an exchange can be made. Just imagine what would it be like if you could learn a skill that helps you secure an income that is 50% greater than what you are currently earning? What would that mean for your life and the lives of your family members and loved ones?

IT'S ABOUT IDENTIFYING AND FACILITATING A WIN-WIN SITUATION

In the previous chapter on Personal Branding, we touched briefly on selling you as a person. This wealth vehicle was about helping you integrate your passion in life with what you do for a living. In that manner, rather than a work-life balance, you would have work-life integration and thus leverage your time. You would do what you love and love what you do while being paid handsomely for it.

With smarter selling, we go beyond that. You don't even need to deliver or develop a product to sell. You can sell something that has already been created and that you believe in. In this way, you can leverage your time by focusing on the sales relationship and transaction, rather than the delivery.

Better yet, you can learn how to sell in front of a room, rather than one-on-one, which is not nearly as time-efficient. Selling one-to-many helps you reap large profits by offering a solution to people's business and life problems. This is exactly what Joel Bauer teaches in his *ProfitPoint* training event. Joel's technique is unique and something that Fortune 500 companies have paid him large sums for in order to build their businesses. Companies such as Microsoft and Apple have benefited from his specialized knowledge. Joel teaches the precise methods for how people can communicate and influence a crowd to buy their offering in a way that serves the needs of the audience.

SMARTER SELLING HELPS YOU LEVERAGE YOUR TIME

The realization of how important learning to sell is came to me when I was working for the shared services cost center of an international firm, Unisys. People from cost centers were regularly being squeezed out or retrenched to save on finances. During that same time, though, salespeople were kept on and highly regarded. Why? Because they brought money in the door, money that helped keep people employed and the company profitable. Most people in back-office or other "secure" jobs that don't require an ability to sell are employed because someone else is doing the selling. Because of that someone, employed people can earn a living, be sheltered, fed, and also support their loved ones and families. At the time, I realized that salespeople were integral to keeping any company afloat and thriving, whereas I was not.

LEARNING TO SELL CAN MAKE YOUR INCOME EARNING ABILITY RECESSION PROOF

Realizing this was life-changing for me. I got out of my comfort zone (I am naturally an introvert) and learned how to sell well. Since then, this skill has served me in establishing business relationships, networking with important people, and building Wealth Mentors to the successful and influential business it is today. Without it, we couldn't have impacted over 12,000 students' financial destinies worldwide since 2003.

WHO IS SELLING BEST SUITED FOR?

Anyone can learn smarter selling if they have the desire. However, it is specifically suited to people who are good at working with the general public and/or willing to move through the resistance that comes with interacting with customers. These people will generally be strong in *Quadrant B* and *Quadrant C*.

To sell requires you to be good at building trust with people, listening to people, perceiving what they really mean despite what they say, and moving them towards a space of mutual understanding. However, if you are strong in the other quadrants, it is not to say you can't *learn* the art of selling and create systems that help you sell without having to interact with people. That's what we will cover in Chapter 8 regarding building a business online. You just might not want to *apply* sales in a face-to-face setting. So please, absorb the knowledge contained here.

Additionally, it also helps if you have a passion for understanding human behavior,

psychology, or generally how and why people behave as they do. You notice funny things, like everyone crowding around the exit door on the bus even though they knew they would all get out, or that people respond to the color red because it is attention-grabbing, or that people respond to words and statements, such as, "don't think of a blue cow," by thinking of one.

IT'S ABOUT COMMUNICATING AND INFLUENCING OTHERS

This skill is priceless if you want to earn a lot of money and be able to do so for life.

1 – Selling Is a Way of Life

The number one reason why I emphasize the need to develop your sales skills and learn how to sell is because selling is life. It's what we as humans do every day whether we know it consciously or not. Selling is not just about pitching a product or service to a consumer in exchange for money; it's about going beyond your comfort zone and interacting with people to reach a desired outcome for both parties. Whether that outcome is to get the job you want, start a relationship with someone you desire, apply for a bank loan, dress to be perceived a certain way, or negotiate a salary, selling permeates every aspect of life.

SELLING IS A PART OF LIFE, WHETHER YOU LIKE IT OR NOT

Just imagine, what would it be like if you knew exactly how to get what you want and make sure that other people get what they want too? What would your life look like? Does it feel very comforting and inspiring? It certainly does for me.

2 – Business Growth and Acceleration

Business growth and profits are dependent on sales and operations. Selling brings in the business, while operations deliver on the sales promise so that customers don't claim cash backs and continue to do business with you. Therefore, your business growth greatly relies on your ability to sell.

WITHOUT A SALE, THERE IS NOTHING TO DELIVER

3 – Branding

Branding is a special type of marketing whereby you can position yourself as the only logical choice in your customer's mind. Selling is an essential skill for branding because it sells an image to your customer that helps them to understand your brand and easily recognize it, and in the best instances, become blind to your competition. Branding is emotional sales using the words, images, and behaviors of your business brand (or personal brand), so that you become the go-to person for a particular product and experience. This generates repeat business which is far less expensive, as it is much easier to sell to a loyal customer than to acquire a new customer (in most cases).

SELLING RIGHT CAN BUILD BRAND LOYALTY

4 – Raising Capital if You Are an Entrepreneur

If you are a budding entrepreneur, then you must learn the art of selling. If you have a business idea and plan to pitch to investors to raise capital, you have to understand how to influence them and create a compelling presentation that promotes the viability of your business plan. Without sales skills, your idea is unlikely to be funded.

Also, if your idea scales to the level that you have to gain agreement from a larger crowd such as the general public (e.g., an Initial Public Offering), you will need to be able to sell the idea and the fact that you and your team of entrepreneurs are the ones to execute it effectively.

RAISING CAPITAL IS ABOUT SELLING YOUR IDEA AND YOUR TEAM

5 – Getting Credit and Loans

If you are a homeowner or budding homeowner, you have to sell your financial credibility to get credit from the banks. The same thing applies to suppliers of credit for business and other things you might invest in or purchase, such as a car. If you don't know how to sell, you will not be able to get good credit.

SMARTER SELLING IS NECESSARY SO PEOPLE UNDERSTAND YOU ARE CAPABLE

6 – Inspiring Management: Your Business Teams

Every CEO, Founder, or Senior Manager knows that in a business, you are selling your business not only to the customers in the marketplace, but to your employees too. You have to communicate clearly how helping you grow your business is going to be beneficial for their personal and professional lives too. As a result, selling is an essential skill to facilitate the process of aligning employee needs with the needs of the company.

Not only do we sell to our employees to retain them, but we also sell to potential employees in the market to inspire the right people to join our business team. You have to sell your business mission, vision, and the compensation you have on offer.

If you can't sell your business mission and vision to your business team, your team will not be able to act with a common, definite purpose.

You also have to manage the challenge that comes with keeping staff motivated and productive, because that directly affects the financial performance and culture of your business.

THE SALES STYLE YOU WANT TO HAVE

In the business world, it's not uncommon for companies and corporations to have a staff of lawyers, or "legal counsel," on retainer to give advice in matters pertaining to the law, taxes, investments, mergers, or other complex or legal situations.

The Counselor knows that when it comes to important buying decisions, customers, be they companies, corporations, or individuals, should all be treated the same. To them, buying any type of product or service is a serious matter and not to be taken lightly. It is an important tool for solving a need, satisfying a problem, or adding to their profits, convenience, or lifestyle. They know that their customers need professional and qualified representation and advice, and the Counselor will do whatever it takes to provide it for them.

Like corporate legal counsel, this salesperson postures him or herself as being "on retainer," always available to give advice on matters pertaining to the products or services they sell. They make it clear in the customer's mind that there is absolutely no need for them to go anywhere else for answers to the problems their products or services can solve.

The Counselor knows how to establish rapport, build professional trust and credibility, identify their customers' current problems, develop effective proposals, offer credible and workable solutions, and make the presentation in such a way that their customers have no question in their minds but that they must buy the concepts they present, and hence, the product or service.

In addition, they have the ability to point out other potential problems that the customer might encounter and help them solve those needs as well. This person operates much like a professional billiards champion. Before each shot, the billiards champion will carefully analyze the layout of the balls on the table to see where the next two or three shots can best be made. Then, with precision, he makes the shot at hand and skillfully directs the cue ball to a predetermined spot so it is poised for the next shot.

Salespeople who function at this skill level also carefully review the customer's needs, both stated and unstated, and skillfully set in motion a plan to address those needs either now, or at a later, more convenient date.

Objections rarely come up because the Counselor has taken the time to anticipate what objections may arise and then builds the answers to the potential objections into his or her presentation.

This salesperson will get every drop of business the customer has, not because of price, but because the customer knows the salesperson really cares about them, understands their needs, and is willing to take the time to identify those needs and offer workable and credible solutions.

PEOPLE DO BUSINESS WITH PEOPLE WHO UNDERSTAND THEM

Getting clear on your potential client's needs also lets you connect how what you have to offer can be valuable to them. Let's go back to the example of a mother who has a passion for healthful cooking and raising her children. If she looked closely at what mothers go through, she might realize that many mothers feel:

- Tight on time.
- Low on energy.
- Overwhelmed by the numerous commitments she has to her family and children.
- Constantly worried whether her child is getting what he/she needs.
- A daily struggle to get their children to eat what's good for them.

Based on the above, if she can somehow create meals that are: simply and quickly made, energizing from a nutrition standpoint, and tasty for children - then she's got a potential income stream!

WHAT CUSTOMERS REALLY WANT

As a business person, it is important for you to understand that only 35% of the reason people buy the product or service you offer is for the actual product or service itself.[1] The other 65% of the reason they buy is for what you can do or provide for them beyond the product or service itself. What the customer really wants to know is: how will I benefit from having you (or your company) involved in my purchase? How are you different from every other vendor out there selling the same or similar product/service?

In today's world, chances are good that your customers and prospects can buy the same product or service (or at least a comparable one) from any one of several of your competitors. With that product or service, your competitor may offer a number of additional advantages as well. They may have a lower price, better quality product, some added bonuses, extra services, a location that's more convenient, or a payment plan that better fits their budget. In today's competitive market, it's difficult to compete on price or product. You may be able to command a certain advantage for a period of time because you have a lower price than your competitors, but you and I both know that it will be short-lived.

It'll just be a matter of time before either one of your competitors lowers their prices or duplicates/improves upon your product. That or you'll need to raise your prices because you no longer have the necessary margins to justify your price. But there's one thing your customers can't get from any of your competitors: You. Your empathy, problem solving expertise, knowledge, education, and a commitment to service that is wholly unique and unable to be replicated.

So, you have to identify the basic motives that make your customers want to buy and honor those motives throughout your sales process. People don't buy for the sake of owning a certain product or service. Rather, they buy because of the benefits they will receive from you as a result of owning that product or service. Remember: 35% versus 65%. Aim high.

WHY PEOPLE BUY

Behavioral psychologists tell us there are seven basic motives that move a person to action and cause them to buy.[2] An understanding of these motives and how they apply to your customers and prospects at the time a buying decision is being made can give you a tremendous advantage.

1. Desire for Gain or Profit

Nobody likes to lose. People want something in return for their efforts and hard work, and the easier they can get it, the better. The success of lottery games in various states bear testimony to people trying to find an easy way to get gain and profit.

If you set things up well, the products you sell can help your customers realize their dreams for gain or profit too. Your customers can and will invest in various types of products or services you sell not to own them, per se, but in an effort to increase their profitability and the amount and value of their assets.

2. Fear of Loss or Need For Security

People will go to great lengths to prevent losing something. A common example: in an effort to protect their property, many people install burglar alarms, fire alarms, smoke detectors, and night lights that automatically come on when movement is detected.

To protect themselves, some people carry spray cans of mace or tear gas, while others have resorted to carrying guns or other weapons.

Psychologists say that the fear of loss or the need for security is perhaps the greatest of all human motives.[3] If the products and services you sell can help protect your clients, their families, or their businesses from loss, or if you can in some way increase their security, either at the present time or sometime in the future, you owe it to them to capitalize on that fact as much and as often as possible.

. . .

3. Pride of Ownership or Status

People want to be noticed and recognized. Little boys ride bicycles with no hands and little girls dress up and act out dance routines and shout to their parents, "Watch me! Watch me!"

Adults do the same things, but in different ways. While they may not verbally shout out, they still say, "Watch me! Watch me!" just as loudly. They do it by the kinds of cars they drive, the clothes and jewelry they wear, the houses they live in, and the material things they possess. One of the benefits of buying certain products is the feeling we get when others see that we own it. In these cases, it's just another way to say, "Watch me! Watch me!"

4. An Interest in Doing Something Easier or More Efficiently

We all want methods of doing things easier. One only has to look around his or her home

to notice the abundance of time and/or money-saving conveniences we all enjoy. What about your products or services? Do they somehow make a person's job, or a business's way of doing things easier or more efficient? And if they do, what are the direct and indirect benefits to your prospect or customer? Is this something you can capitalize on?

5. The Desire to Be Engaged

Abraham Maslow placed human needs into five sequential categories:[4]

1. Physiological needs (e.g., food and shelter)
2. Safety needs (e.g., personal protection, family safety, and belongings)
3. Social needs (e.g., love, friendships, sexual relationships)

4. Self needs (e.g., feel confidence)
5. Self-actualizing needs (e.g., personal growth, purpose)

He argued that people's needs in one category must be met before they can turn their attention to the next, such as safety first before self-actualization. However, there is something *much* more powerful that drives human behavior: the *need* to be mentally engaged.

Political organizations use it to program their people into hate-filled frenzies. They understand that people have a desperate need for mental engagement, to have their attention captured, focused, and intensified. Hitler was well aware of this need, and in filling it for his followers, he led an army to slaughter millions of lives.

It doesn't appear on Maslow's scale and may not replace those needs identified earlier. However, the need to be mentally engaged *overrides* them. Think about how many times you have heard the phrase, "I'd rather be dead than bored" or "I'm dead bored." People can't handle boredom. But if we are engaged, we can be starving and searching for food, and before we know it, something can capture our full attention and hours can pass without any sensation of hunger.

Artists and musicians know this. We can be in severe pain and without being aware of it, something captures our attention and the pain is temporarily gone. We've all experienced situations like these, especially as kids, where the *time* seemed to fly. Every moment of each day, we want to be engaged by something. People seek entertainment.

Even if people are exhausted and want to relax, we simply engage in something else to help *unwind*. All this in an effort to alleviate the one thing few people can settle with: boredom.

6. Self-Improvement and Personal Growth

Your investment of both money and time in this book is a good example of your desire for self-improvement and increased effectiveness. People want and need to improve and be able to do things more efficiently. Sometimes that involves taking risks with time or money. but not all risks have to be "risky." Calculated risks based on well-thought-out plans and outcomes are the safest way to go and can contribute greatly to the successful improvement in effectiveness and efficiency.

7. The Desire for Importance or the Need to Feel Appreciated

According to noted psychiatrist Dr. Abraham Maslow, acceptance and appreciation are two of the most basic needs of all humans. Children want to be accepted by their parents and peers, and parents want their children to remember them when they grow up and leave home.

In his book, *The Human Side of Enterprise,* Douglas McGregor explains that workers are motivated more by "significant works," and a feeling of being needed and appreciated, than by money.[5]

People want to make a difference and be appreciated for it. Fathers and mothers not only have an obligation to see that their family's futures are provided for, but they want their family to understand and appreciate their efforts. Business owners have an obligation to the people who buy from them, the employees who work for them, their employees' families, their suppliers, and the vendors who sell to them. Too often, though, each of those groups of people live with an attitude of expectancy and entitlement. That is, they expect that the business owner will take care of them. How much easier would life be if more appreciation were shown to those who make our lives better?

If the products or services you provide the marketplace can help make any or all of these possible, you may have an open ticket to success because of the great, unsatisfied need that exists. If you understand these basic motives and how they apply to your product or service-based business, then use them to sell to the needs (both stated and unstated) of your customers. Both you and your customer will prosper from it.

If you are not prospering, it simply means you have not uncovered your customers' motives for buying. You are not addressing their specific needs. In most cases, you can't wait for your customers to tell you what they want; you have to be able to recognize their needs. Remember, you are ultimately responsible for the success or failure of your business. If you are doing it right or wrong, either way, the marketplace will let you know.

THE LOYALTY OF THE CUSTOMER IS PRICELESS

Customers make an interesting study. It seems that they always want the very most for the very least. They are ruthless, selfish, demanding, and disloyal. You know the story. You've done business with someone for several years, and they've been a good customer. You've given them the best service possible and think they are your customer for life. But then some little thing goes wrong, or they see an ad for someone else, or they get a call from a competitor (someone they've never met before, with a slightly lower price), and the next thing you know, they are gone, oftentimes without a single word to you.

At first, you don't notice it. But one day you realize that it's been a while since you've seen or heard from that customer. When you find out what happened, you feel bad, because if they would have just called you, you might have been able to make a couple of changes and save the business. But it's too late; they're gone.

This scenario is repeated time and again with business owners from every company, who sell every type of product or service. It is going to happen. To pretend that it doesn't, or won't happen, is simply deceiving yourself. It's incredible how many business owners just write off the loss of a good customer. But that's not what you should do. Instead, now is the time to become even more proactive and go after that "lost" customer.

One of the best ways to minimize or cut down on the frequency of losing your good customers is to resell them on the reasons they bought from you in the first place. Regularly scheduled meetings or conversations with your customers to remind them of their motives can go a long way in helping insulate your business from the competition. Remember: your competition has similar products, services, and prices. Also remember that your customer's reasons for buying are only 35% based on those products, services, and prices. The other 65% is for what you can do for them.

Spend time with them. Review their needs, wants, and concerns. Remind them why they bought from you in the first place. Reinforce their motives and their decisions for buying, and you will reduce your customer defection rate and develop not only loyal customers but friends as well.

8

BUILDING YOUR BUSINESS ONLINE

"The richest people in the world look for and build networks; everyone else looks for work."
— Robert Kiyosaki

Building a business online is not new anymore. If you are in business, it is necessary. It is also a great opportunity if you want to accumulate wealth by leveraging your time, scaling your revenue to a global market, and generally enjoying location freedom too. Just imagine what it would be like if you could launch a product within a matter of hours and earn yourself an income from the comfort of, well, wherever your computer is?!

What if you could find a market that you are passionate about and earn money by sharing that with a global audience who is waiting and hanging on to every word you say? Better yet, what if, on the internet alone, you could create multiple streams of income with a mindset and approach that you can duplicate time after time, to generate massive revenue?

If you are already in an offline business, what if, by properly using an internet platform, you could cut costs dramatically, increase revenue like never before, and reduce the amount of long-term time input on your behalf? What would that mean for your life?

WELCOME TO THE WONDERFUL WORLD OF INTERNET BUSINESS!

That's what's possible if you learn the ways of doing business on the internet. If you learn the right ways, that have been proven to work, you could reap the following benefits:

- **Enjoy unlimited location and time freedom** – so you can earn money wherever you are, whoever you are with, and whenever you would like. If that is with your family, traveling the world, and potentially only working a few hours a day, perfect!
- **Uncapped income potential** – because of the global nature of the internet, you can gain customers from the billions of people worldwide.
- **Sustainable income** – because you can enter any specialty market you would like, using the timeless business principles, you will always be able to find opportunities to capitalize on, and hedge your risk by not putting all your eggs in one basket.
- **Do what you love to do** – because the internet is a platform for doing business, you can express what you love and use the many business models available online, to earn money doing that. That way, it can be both profitable and fulfilling.
- **Small budget to start and operate a business** – with a computer and connection to the internet, you can start an online business with as little as a few hundred

dollars. This is a great way to learn and earn with minimal financial risk if you are just starting out!

- **Earn money while you sleep** – by using automated sales, marketing, and delivery processes, you can earn a lot of money "hands-off."

These are just some of the benefits you stand to gain. The important thing to note is that once you learn the proper ways of doing business on the internet, the opportunities are endless, which means you can tailor your business activities to suit the lifestyle you want. You can leverage your talents and natural strengths to make this work. That is critical for creating and sustaining wealth.

WEALTH THAT HONORS YOUR WAY OF LIFE

Cindy had to take care of her handicapped child at home but struggled to find the time and money to raise her child, as she had to work her day job as a financial planner as well. The only way she could work to generate sales was to take her child along with her in her car as she went from meeting to meeting. As you can imagine, it was really tough on her and her child. Learning internet marketing from Derek Gehl (our internet marketing and online business guru) allowed Cindy to work more from home, generate a couple of thousand dollars per month, and care for her child and family. She applied her sales skills and her financial skills to earn more money online, and in the comfort of her own space. Rather than being stressed out and stuck in peak-hour traffic, she created the space for the more important things in her life: family.

"When I first started Derek's program I was a complete beginner. Now I've developed my own website and am selling my own eBook online. Making money online is actually not that hard! This is the best training program that I've ever joined!"

— Tiffany Chung, Singapore

In this chapter, I am going to draw upon my personal experience and Derek Gehl's knowledge of online businesses to share with you the mindset and mechanisms that are required for a successful online business.

There is a problem though: because the internet is not new anymore, the market has become increasingly noisy about what works for generating an income and what doesn't. I only recommend a training program after I have personally tested multiple systems from different trainers worldwide. It always comes down to one thing…

WHAT RESULTS DO THESE TRAINERS GET FOR THEIR STUDENTS?

Results don't lie.

You can have fancy marketing and make false promises and have people ready to buy. But the truth is, if someone has helped thousands of people grow their own successful online businesses (e.g. at least $100,000 per year) and has sold a successful online business and marketing course for over ten years consistently, then something that he/she is sharing, works. Better yet, if their own internet business has made over $60 million in sales online, then you want to pay attention. To top it off, if I have personally used the system to build my online business and have seen many of my own clients succeed in business using the exact same system, then you will really want to pay attention.

Well, that system exists. It is taught and shared by our world-renowned trainer Derek Gehl, who reveals decades of expertise in the online space to allow people to build the lifestyle they want and take care of their families, very much like what Derek has done for himself back in Canada. He has a wife and children and lives by the mountains where he can care for his family and pursue his passion for mountain biking too.

Next, I will touch on the skills and traits that are of natural benefit when it comes to doing business online. I will also share some of Derek's knowledge so you can really get your head around how the internet works and how it could work in your favor. Please note that just as business is diverse in skill sets that are useful, so too is doing business online. Somewhere and somehow, your natural strengths will be useful in this domain called the internet.

It all comes down to understanding what you are most passionate about, what strengths you have to offer, and choosing the right online business model to express that. This will be covered in more detail as we dive deeper into the content of this chapter, but before we do, it is important you get clear on your natural strengths and purpose.

"When I first started I had my own website but I did not know how to make it rank well in search engines. Now nearly half of the business for one division of my company is through my website. If someone asks me if I recommend Derek's program, my answer is a definite YES!"

— Kwan Ka Pang, Kuala Lumpur, Malaysia

VERY IMPORTANT REMINDER

It never hurts to drive this key point home: the internet itself is not a business. I see this too often. People think that "getting online" means they are in business, which simply isn't true. It is like saying that walking into a shopping mall means you are in business. The internet is a platform that allows us to run different types of businesses. Just like shopping centers facilitate different operations for a variety of businesses, the internet is a platform with huge potential that facilitates businesses of all natures.

So if you choose to learn the business of doing business online, you are not only learning about the internet as a platform, and how it operates and evolves over time, you are essentially learning business. In this chapter, whether you are in an online business or not, you will learn things that will add more dimensions to your understanding of all business today.

INTERNET BUSINESS MANTRA

"The money is in the list," is a line you will never get sick of hearing if you are doing business online. But what does it mean? Business online is not simply about creating a product/service and selling it. The most valuable asset as your business grows is not your product, website, or any technologies; it is your list.

A list contains the names and contacts of people who find you of value and want to hear more from you. In a traditional business sense, it means you have a large number of people who trust you, value you, and have a positive emotional attachment to who you are as a business and individual. As you know, that means they will likely buy whatever you recommend, because people buy from people they trust!

ONLINE BUSINESS IS ABOUT BUILDING A DATABASE OF PEOPLE WHO TRUST YOU

This is a huge thing. It means having a potentially eternal, repeat customer base that can pay you for the rest of your life! Think about it. Say I lost everything from a product or service perspective because the market shifted and no longer valued those things. Say I even lost my computer and access to my office because of some mishap. Even if all these things happen, I could easily enter an internet café, get online, find a new niche or market online, set up my online systems, and directly market to my list to earn money. Within a matter of hours or even days, I could be earning money and be back on my feet again.

BUILDING A DATABASE CAN PAY YOU FOR LIFE

In traditional business, the equivalent is the number and quality of relationships you have with business partners and customers because word of mouth is one of the best ways to grow your business. Now that the internet allows you to connect and access a global market, it is like word of mouth on super steroids!

8 DIFFERENT BUSINESS MODELS YOU CAN USE ONLINE

Since we are talking about the business of doing business online, it is worth giving you an overview of the different business models you can use on the internet. These are not set in stone because the internet is always evolving and, like every business, you can diversify and create a hybrid of business models (recommended) to earn money and succeed in the long term. However, it helps to frame things up, so you can understand the different ways that people are already earning money online. Those methods and mindsets will be useful when business online evolves into the future. Here are some different models you can use on the internet (I attribute these to Derek Gehl):

. . .

1 – Authority Blog

The authority blog targets a specific niche. In case you don't know, a niche is, in essence, a very narrowed down audience with highly specific traits. For example, instead of targeting the relatively wide niche of "bookkeeping service providers," you might target bookkeepers who are also partners of mid-tier law firms within Australia, who focus on family law. The authority blog shares useful content in the form of an online website and blog and connects to a specific group of people who would find that content useful and/or fascinating. If it is useful content to them, they will opt-in to your list because they will want to keep hearing from you.

Of course, by giving upfront value to those readers or subscribers, you build trust with that following. Over time, you have the opportunity to monetize that. People who offer a product or service that your niche might find useful will want to pay you to advertise on your site. Alternatively, you could grab an affiliate product and recommend that to your following (a product you don't create or own, but by selling it on behalf of someone, you receive a % commission). That might be a holiday package or a massage and therapeutic product, but whatever it is, as long as it is of value to your audience, they are more likely to buy it from you than someone else because they trust you.

This is huge. Not only do you have the potential to earn more money from big brands who want access to your following, but you also gain a list of trusted subscribers who are looking to you for direction. The cycle is as follows.

ADD VALUE – BUILD A FOLLOWING – MONETIZE

Question is, is this something that attracts you? Can you see yourself creating content and sharing it online? Does it come naturally to you?

. . .

2 – Membership Website

A membership site is where people can buy access to your website and specialized content and skills in exchange for money on a regular subscription. Think about a membership structure in a traditional offline business, such as a gym. People pay money in weekly or monthly installments to access gym classes and equipment. The same thing happens with a membership site; people pay to access valuable content that can, in some way or another, enhance their life or solve a problem they have. The beauty of a membership (versus selling a digital product) is that you can create an online community and deepen the relationship you have with your list while continuing to add value and secure an ongoing revenue stream month to month (or week to week). Again, it's about building and preserving that list!

3 – E-Books and Videos

By creating an electronic book or video that is useful for a particular niche, you can have people pay to download it. Even better, if it is of tremendous value, they might share it with their friends and family. In this way, you can earn money hands-off, assuming your systems are set up properly. This is an online representation of a very simple business principle: where people pay a once-off fee for a product or service, such as buying a book from a bookstore or buying a DVD from a video store. This is easier to set up than a membership site, and you could become profitable from single sales revenues very quickly.

4 – Review Site

Similar to a blog, it is focused on a niche that gives an opinion or review about a certain line of products or services.

The reason this is of value to people is that before people buy things online, they like doing their research and discovering what other people are saying about a particular product or service. The primary question being, "Does this work for other people?"

By doing reviews, you can create an affiliate link to the product or service you are reviewing. If someone buys the product, you earn a commission. Once your review is up and traffic is drawn towards it, you could be earning money with little additional effort. Again, always review a particular niche and narrow it down. Don't just pick skincare. Pick a particular aspect of skincare, such as acne, eyeliner for working professionals, or organic men's hair gel.

5 – E-Commerce Website

This is a shopping cart-style website that sells physical products (think Amazon.com). There is a lot of money to be made selling physical products online. The last time I checked, it is one of the biggest growth sectors because people are looking to buy physical products online more than ever before. That means by choosing a niche, you can build an e-commerce website and start earning money online. Compared to a traditional physical store that sells T-shirts for male teens in a local area, you can set one up online and sell them to the world. This is especially valuable if you are bringing an overseas product into some local markets, where those local markets would normally pay a significant premium for shipping costs.

IT'S ABOUT BRINGING VALUE TO YOUR CONSUMERS

By setting up an e-commerce store, you can also display multiple products on offer and upsell them to customers to increase the dollar value per customer.

. . .

6 – Third Party Platforms

This is where it gets interesting. Third-party platforms help you to set up your online shop using their platform. Once that is done, you can start selling their products but branded as your business. Go see what Amazon does. They allow anybody to open their own e-Commerce website on their platform and sell their products. They started with books, but have diversified immensely. So the opportunity to generate an income is huge. Amazon has millions and millions of shoppers! And they aren't the only ones. eBay does it too. Though they started with auctions for products, people are now going there to buy fixed-price goods. The great thing about these platforms is that you can acquire customers from a space that is already highly trafficked, sell products you don't have to create or own yourself, build an email list following for your particular niche, and then bring them to your own website and nurture them for the long run. Again, the wealth is in your list!

7 – Services

We covered online e-commerce sites that ship physical goods, but if you are providing a service you might consider using platforms that sell your service (e.g. web design, consulting, writing, etc...). Some good examples are O-Desk, E-Lance, and Fiverr. By providing professional services online and registering yourself with these platforms, you can earn more money by reaching a larger market that is in demand for your service. Better yet, you aren't limited to your own country!

8 – Hybrid

A hybrid is a combination of multiple business models. This

is where your business eventually evolves to a point of capitalizing on the use of numerous ways of doing online business (eg., using one or more of the seven I have provided above). You could sell an ebook and then move your customers from the ebook to a membership site, where you provide live support and updated training, relevant to the content you have sold them before. You can do this to strengthen the community and your following. Later on, you might also sell them physical products that complement what you are teaching them or even a high-end personalized consultation (service offering) for those that are serious about working with you one-on-one.

To give you a simple comparison, suppose you are a baker who isn't online. Using a hybrid offline business model, you could sell bread directly to consumers from your shop, but you could also have a delivery service that sells bulk orders to cafes and restaurants in your district, and on the side, you could run live workshops that teach people the art of baking. Your business is not limited to a single revenue stream!

Like any business, the key is to diversify and create a hybrid of business models to earn money and succeed in the long term. You don't have to look at the previous seven ways of making money as individual pillars. Rather, you can mix and match to what suits your business niche and market.

"When I started with Derek I was a complete newbie. Now I have developed my own product and managed to set up two websites that generate passive income. If someone asked me if I would recommend Derek's training I would say YES!"
— Aaric Niew, Kuala Lumpur, Malaysia

THE 6-STEP PROCESS TO MARKETING YOUR BUSINESS ONLINE

Keeping in mind the importance of building a list every time we talk about online business and the different business models you can use to generate an income online, I am going to share with you the 6-step process that Derek Gehl uses to market businesses online. These are the same steps that we use at Wealth Mentors to bring thousands of people into our live events and trainings, and which led to our business being voted Promising SME in 2012. Remember, a business is about providing value to the market and staying profitable by making sure that what you receive is greater than the input (cost) to produce that value.

Step 1 – Uncover Your Niche Market

Firstly, you need to confirm that there is a need for whatever it is your business is going to sell and that people are willing to pay for it! Doing market research before you set up a business is just as important in the online world as it is offline. Online research tools now make it incredibly easy and affordable to do this kind of research.

The term "niche market" is one that you will hear in just about every discussion regarding business and marketing, both offline and online. But it is important to understand that people think of niches in different ways. Traditional markets define a niche market as a large group of people sharing several characteristics. For example, men aged 30-35 years of age and earning between US$50K and US$75K per year. However, online niches are very different. They are much narrower and far more targeted.

A Niche is a Group of People Searching the Internet for a Solution to a Problem but Are Yet to Find Many Relevant Search Results

Building an online business is like building a house: every piece supports the rest of the structure, and it all relies on a strong foundation. The foundation of every great business (online or offline), is a solid "niche market." Identifying your niche is one of the biggest challenges you will face before choosing a product (or products) to market to that niche. Often, people ask Derek Gehl at his internet marketing seminars, "Derek, what is the best product to sell online?" Now, this sounds like a fair question, but it is a big mistake that most new online businesses make!

Rather than asking what product to sell online, it is about finding a targeted niche of people with a common problem so that you can offer a range of products and solutions. This is smarter business. But it begs the question, how do you know who your potential customers are? How do you find them? How do you determine if you have a niche market? The formula below will help you.

"My niche market is people who are [insert action] + [your area of interest]"

For example: my niche market is musicians (type of people) who are looking to play (action) a set of African conga drums (area of interest). Another one might be parents who are looking to build a treehouse for their children.

Now that you understand how to define your niche: how do you find out if it will be profitable? How do you connect with the people inside it? Simple, use a keyword research tool to discover exactly what people are searching for online.

These tools allow you to discover the exact keywords people

type into search engines (Google, Yahoo, etc.) when they're trying to find information. Note, "Keywords" are simply the words and phrases searchers use to describe what they're looking for online. These tools not only help you identify your niche, but they show you how many sites are competing for those terms, which effectively allows you to research your competition. Nice, right? Based on your search results (for example, the number of people who might be searching for "hot pink glitter nail polish"), you will be able to determine how much traffic your site could expect in any 24-hour period. It would be like running a café and knowing exactly how busy you are going to get!

There are many keyword tools to use, so feel free to have a look around. However, the two that I have seen work the best are:

- Keyword Discovery
- Wordtracker

Both these keyword tools offer "free trial" versions that will give you an idea of how they work and the kind of information they provide. However, when you are ready to dive fully into the research phase of your online business, we always recommend using the paid version of any keyword research tool. To truly know if your niche is viable, you're going to want to get as much keyword information as you can.

INFORMATION IS KING

Keyword research tools also allow you to find out how many people may be searching for information to solve a particular problem, which in turn, is a representation of demand for your product, service, or solutions. They will also give you an idea of the competition you have in the market, so you can determine the likelihood of success or the level of risk associated with a particular business venture. If you are strong in *Quadrant C* and *Quadrant D*, then this will be an activity you will ace.

Step 2 – Make Sure to Sell the Right Solution

Now it is time to come up with a product or service that does a good job of satisfying the need you've identified in Step 1. Because no matter how good your marketing or your niche is, it won't last long if you don't provide good value.

Therefore, before you even market your product to your niche, you must make sure to find a solution that truly satisfies and matches their needs. You don't want to waste time and money investing in something that no one is interested in buying, and worse yet, something that the people who buy will be greatly disappointed in.

As covered earlier in this chapter, there are lots of ways to make money online and serve your niche. These include: developing and selling your own product, selling your services, selling information products, dropshipping with an e-commerce site, affiliates, etc. The possibilities are endless, but you need to start with one. So after getting clear on your niche, I would advise going back to the eight different business models described earlier in this chapter and picking the one that you'd like to get started on.

FOCUS ON THE POWER OF ONE

After you get a degree of success with one business vehicle online, you can start to look at combining profit streams (the Hybrid model) to explode your income potential. The key is to focus on one, maximize the amount of revenue you get from it, and then move on to the next. Combining income streams gives you the opportunity to generate more money than would ever be possible with a single profit strategy. It also helps protect your business income against fluctuations in the marketplace.

You see, any business is prone to slow periods and forces beyond our control, so it is always a good idea to avoid putting all your eggs in one basket. Suppose a lot of your income comes from booking skiing trips for tourists in Switzerland, but one year, winter comes late, and there is virtually no snow (weather is something we can't control). You may still sell some vacation packages, but you are not going to get anywhere near the type of revenue you were looking for.

However, what if you sold ebooks that told people about the best skiing locations on the continent and marketed it as providing options when your favorite skiing spot just doesn't seem to hold up for that year? What if you sold an ebook on how to have a fun alternative to a skiing holiday, one that you can use all-year-round? To top it off, with your vacation sales site, you could generate affiliate income by also promoting skis, snowboards, and snow gear.

IT'S ALL ABOUT RELEVANCE AND VALUE

So even though your main source of income might take a big hit, you can still generate income from other sources that would help sustain your business revenues until the next season. Once you've set up one profitable business, you can take what you've learned and use it to build another one, in much less time. Again, the trick to building a successful, multifaceted business is to take things one step at a time.

Start with one sales model and then tweak and test it until it generates maximum profits. Then you can conduct more research into your market to discover what other products or services they'd like you to offer, and then add them to your business. Of course, there is a lot of information you'll have to learn in order to build your business as efficiently as possible. This kind of knowledge doesn't just come to you overnight.

Step 3 – Keep Your Visitors Glued to Your Site

Whether your site is a shopping cart, a blog, or an online service-oriented website, you are going to need compelling sales copy to keep your visitors glued to your site: firstly, for them to be able to understand the message you are trying to get across, but more importantly, to have them take action based on that message.

When you are doing business online, the words on your site become the equivalent of your salesperson (when compared to traditional business). The only contact you're going to have with the vast majority of your potential customers is through the text on your website, your sales copy.

So when we are talking about sales copy, we do not mean big headlines or five-word blurbs that most websites use online in the hope that it will generate sales. What we are referring to are carefully constructed words that take your visitor by the hand and lead them through all the necessary steps in your sales process. Before anyone makes a purchase online or offline or takes an action, they need to know what's in it for them and that they have more to gain than not.

In some cases, short chunks of text that detail your products will be enough to persuade visitors to click through to product pages; but in most cases, you will need long-form copy in order to sell. Generally speaking, long sales copy works best for sites that sell one product or service, while shorter copy works best for "catalog-style sites" that sell a number of different products, such as an e-commerce website.

So you have to make sure the words do a great job of selling your product or service. Compelling sales copy should do the following:

- **Immediately draw the reader** in with exciting benefits and enticing copy so you can lead them toward the sale.
- **Establish your credibility and trust** since nobody will buy from you if they don't think they can trust you, or at least relate to you.
- **Explain the benefits** of your product or service to the reader and show why they need it.
- **Direct visitors through the sales process** in a way that encourages the maximum number of sales.
- **Address all their key concerns** as consumers are skeptical these days. Most likely, they have already been exposed to a lot of hyped-up, false promises elsewhere and want to know that you are different.

THE BEST COPY IS COST-EFFECTIVE AND LEVERAGES YOUR TIME

If the copy is done well, your "virtual salesperson" is highly cost-effective and able to work on your business while you sleep!

Salesmanship is also a critical skill for copywriting. It is therefore worth learning and absorbing what was shared in Chapter 7, so you can get a solid understanding of what true sales or smarter selling is. It is, in every sense, a skill for life.

Below are some tips for writing compelling sales copy for any online business. You don't necessarily have to do it yourself. In fact, unless you're a copywriter, I will always recommend outsourcing it. But it does help to have a basic understanding of what good copy does so that you can do some quality control when you hire professional copywriters to help you.

Tip 1 – Your Unique Selling Proposition

Successful sales copy will position your product offer from a unique sales angle. What is your 'Unique Selling Proposition' (USP)? What is the most attractive aspect of your product or service? For example, if you are selling toasters, what makes your toaster different from all the other toasters out there, and is that difference of value to your consumer?

For a service such as FedEx, the promise (and USP) is, "we get it there overnight" – something that no other mail carrier could do in the marketplace at the time. A good way to fine-tune your unique selling proposition is by asking yourself:

HOW DOES MY PRODUCT OR SERVICE DO A BETTER JOB THAN OTHERS?

Tip 2 – Get Clear on Your Target Reader

Defining your market is a critical step in the early stages of setting up your online business. Once you have it defined, it is necessary to understand how to best communicate with them. You have to understand whether you are speaking to: a teenager in New York City, surfers on the Sunshine Coast of Australia, someone in a Singaporean-based small-business, or an executive of a multinational organization?

The language, focus, and value will be vastly different for each audience. Just as in real life, you speak differently to an engineer than you would to your hairdresser, not because of some social hierarchy, but simply because we all perceive the world differently. It's natural for us to modify our communication so that we can better understand each other. You wouldn't speak to a toddler the same as a senior citizen, would you?

TO BE UNDERSTOOD, YOU NEED TO KNOW WHO IT IS YOU ARE TALKING TO

Other bits of information that may help you get into their world include understanding the primary concerns or challenges that they want to overcome and relating to their key emotional states. What gets them excited or concerned?

You don't just have to guess. The best way is to go out and ask by conducting some market research or running a survey so that you can discover the reasons that people will buy a particular product or service. Trust me, some of them may have never occurred to you!

Tip 3 – An Attention-Grabbing Headline

No matter what subject matter your website addresses, you can benefit from a compelling headline on your homepage. People are busy and life is busy, so you have to grab their attention. One of the best ways to get their attention is to communicate the biggest benefit of your product or the biggest problem that your product resolves to attract enough interest to draw readers to find out more.

Let me give you an example: "Sore Knee Relief – 3 Easy Steps!" Yes, it sounds "salesy," but if you are struggling specifically with knee pain, it will likely get your attention and leave you wanting to find out more. Again, it is all about relevance. In general, a really good headline should accomplish all or some of the following:

- Emphasize the key benefit
- Emphasize the biggest solution
- Generate curiosity and pull visitors to want to find out more

- Capture the essence of the main attractions or *power* of your product or service

Once you've written a few headlines, test them. Run them for a couple of weeks, then compare the results with other headlines.

IT IS A COMBINATION OF EDUCATED GUESSING AND RIGOROUS TESTING

Tip 4 – Establish Credibility

People are skeptics, even more so online. If given a chance, most of us will always find an excuse not to buy a product or service. So, establishing credibility and building a degree of trust is critical if you are to be the solution for them. You can establish your credibility in a couple of different ways.

1. **Explain what makes you an "expert"** in your field by providing information about your experience whether in terms of working years, achievements, awards, or other forms of recognition.
2. **Provide customer testimonials** because the proof is in the pudding, so to speak. Plus, because people live vicariously through the words and actions of others, a testimonial could provide them with enough reasons to want to make a purchase. If they can relate to what is being said, readers will be more convinced by what your customers have to say about your product, than by what you have to say about it, guaranteed.

Tip 5 – Communicate the Benefits

This is a key distinction: do not communicate the features of your products, rather, communicate the benefits of your product. There is a subtle difference:

- **A feature** is one of the components or functions of your product or service (e.g., A hand drill has three different sized drills that can be fitted to the front).
- **A benefit** is something your product or service will do for your buyer. (e.g., A hand drill creates a hole in the wall within a matter of seconds).

Tip 6 – A Guarantee

If you are confident with your product or service, then you should not be afraid to back it up with a guarantee. For example, you could offer a "no questions asked, lifetime money-back guarantee." You might be thinking that this is risky, right? Well, you might be surprised. Did you know the longer the guarantee is good for, the fewer requests for returns you get?

It's a fact. Here's why: the consumer feels confident that your product or service will live up to its promises, and they don't feel rushed to return your product. With a longer return period, they will keep putting it off, and the pressure on them is off.

Tip 7 – Provide a Free Bonus

If your package communicates value that far exceeds what your customers expect to pay, you can pile on even more, so that they will hardly believe that you are being so generous to them. It becomes a near "no brainer" in their mind. The easiest way to do this is by creating a package of free bonuses that, combined with the value of the product itself, is perceived to be worth much more than the price they are being asked for.

When you're deciding what to offer as a free bonus, your options are almost limitless, but here are a few basic rules to follow:

1. Make sure that the bonus is of value to your target market. For example, if your offering is travel-related, you might offer complimentary tickets for a VIP lounge at the airport.
2. Choose something that is related to your product or service that will enhance your offering in some way. For example, if it is travel-related, you might give them a complimentary ebook or a product that helps with jet lag.

Tip 8 – Create a Sense of Urgency

Almost everyone is great at putting things off until "later." It is the same when it comes to sales. Even if your sales copy has them convinced, they could still say "maybe I'll come back and check it out later," which means they won't because they will likely forget. So you must create a sense of urgency to prompt them to take action immediately. You can do this in a few different ways:

- **Limit the time** for which your offer is available.
- **Limit the quantity** of products or services you can offer.
- **Offer a discount** for those who take action now, and within a certain time frame.
- **Add even more bonuses** for a limited time, if they take action immediately.

Tip 9 – A Strong Call to Action

Ask for the business. It's that simple. All the steps you have taken to create compelling copy are useless unless you ask for the business. You have to spell it out as clearly as possible: how your reader can order your product or service and what action they must take. It may seem obvious, but you need to spell it out. Here are a few examples of simple, but direct, ways of asking for the order:

- Click here to order now
- Buy now (on a button)
- To order your copy, along with your bonuses – click here now

Just as in a shopping center, there is a counter where your payment is processed, and the person serving you will ask you for the amount of money and the method of processing payment.

Tip 10 – Your Contact Information

This is often overlooked. Once you have asked for the order, it is important you make it easy for your customers to contact you. Whether this is via a secure online form, phone number, or email address (or all three), potential customers may sometimes have questions they want answered before committing to your offer. It's also a great way to help your buyer feel "secure" about their purchase, even if they have no questions pre-purchase. Just knowing that they can contact you later (even if they never do) will help them feel safe in buying from you.

Also, personalize the experience as much as possible. People feel better talking to people if you say: "Contact this number and ask for Nick" than if you say, "call this number to speak to a representative".

STEP 4 – DESIGN A WEBSITE THAT LEADS VISITORS TO TAKE ACTION

A storefront that has class, simplicity, and function can be the difference between a bustling business and an empty one. This principle holds true for online businesses too. But rather than having someone walk in your store and delivering an experience of service and convenience through physical architecture, it is about giving the user the best experience when clicking and navigating through your virtual architecture – your website. Unfortunately, most small online businesses tend to commit fatal design errors that drive their visitors away within seconds of arriving at their site.

Here are some simple tips to get your site right:

- **Grab people on the first page** – and above the fold (that is, what they see immediately without having to scroll down). At first sight, they should be able to judge if what you have is of relevance to them or not. This includes what you do, benefits you deliver, unique selling points, and even a testimonial. Help them judge you correctly!
- **Plan your website in advance** – using pencil and paper. That way, you can see exactly what you need to provide, rather than adding as you go. One simple way to plan effectively is to decide what tabs are needed. Tabs are the clickable menus (or pages) that are usually located alongside the banner of your computer.
- **Don't overdo the graphics** – unless they support the message you are trying to get across or support the sale.
- **Keep it as simple as possible** – the fewer clicks it takes to get to something your customer wants, the

better. If they want to buy a product, don't make them go through a tedious process for payment. It will turn them off!

While every site is different, here are a few basic pages (tabs) your visitors will expect to see as part of a standard and credible website. If you visit sites like Amazon and eBay, you will see they include most, if not, all of the following:

- **Frequently Asked Questions (FAQs)** – this is where you list the most common questions your visitors ask and provide the answers. Not only does this give your visitors the information they are looking for, but it also allows you to address customer concerns or objections, and minimize the time and money spent on customer service (answering and responding to inquiries).
- **Privacy Statement** – Privacy is a sensitive issue, and you need to assure your visitors that you will respect theirs. To do this, some of the things you will need to outline in your privacy statement are: what sort of information you collect from each visitor, what you do with it, who you share it with, and whether you use cookies. Transparency is important.
- **Terms of service (or Acceptable Use Policy)** – this is a set of guidelines that outline the terms and conditions of your site and can be thought of as your "rules" for online behavior. For example, if you have a membership site, you could use this policy to state what sort of conduct is unacceptable in your chat rooms or member forums. If someone were to abuse the policy, you can state the consequences of such actions. This section also covers any legal statements, warranties, or disclaimers that you have. To get a

sense of what they might be, take a look at a few credible websites that are similar to your own.

- **About us** – People want to know who they are dealing with. This page allows you to share the background and story of your site, business, and yourself. It goes a long way in establishing trust. It's also useful to include a picture of yourself, any key team members, and to spell out exactly what your site is aiming to do.
- **Contact us** – visitors should be able to easily find your mailing address, telephone number, and/or contact form. Where possible, provide a name for contact, as people generally feel more comfortable when there is a name attached to a specific title. So even if you have delegated the role of customer service and call inquiries to someone else, make sure you list their name(s) as well.
- **Shopping cart** – if your site offers multiple products or services, your customers will expect a "shopping cart." This helps them to collect various products from your site until they are ready to purchase. It's all about providing service to your shoppers and making it as easy as possible to buy everything they need!

STEP 5 – CAPTURE LEADS TO BUILD CUSTOMER RELATIONSHIPS

If you only set up your website to sell a product, then you could be missing out on more than 80% of the sales you could be making. Why? Because the vast majority of online shoppers don't make a purchase on their first visit to a website. Most people need a minimum of 7-8 points of contact with a business before they feel comfortable enough to buy.

If you don't reach out and give them a compelling reason

why they should give you their contact information, and then stay in touch with them, build a relationship, and overcome their buyer resistance, then you'll never realize your full income potential.

So, how exactly do you stay in touch with them and build trust so they feel comfortable enough to buy from you? The answer is elementary: via an "opt-in." By using "opt-in" forms to capture people's contacts in the form of a list (email address and names), you position yourself to be able to build customer relationships for the long run. Remember: the power of online business is in your list! In this way, you can increase the amount of future revenue you gain, and of course, increase the value per customer.

There was a time when email opt-ins (in exchange for a freebie) were a huge thing. Nowadays, this has evolved into other sophisticated ways to engage and build your audience. Some commonly used examples are Facebook fan pages, YouTube channels, Twitter, and LinkedIn.

IT'S ABOUT BUILDING A DATABASE OF PEOPLE WHO TRUST YOU

The principle stays the same: people buy from people they know and trust. By capturing leads and engaging with them regularly through some form of media (e.g., email, video, blog), you can build those relationships. You can create a brand identity for your business and position yourself as the go-to expert in your client's (and potential client's) mind.

There are many methods to provide incentives for someone to opt-in. Of course, some people might like your blog content so much they will want to opt-in just to hear from you. Other methods include free ebook giveaways, access to free training, or even an "enter-to-win" contest! It is up to you to choose which one is best for the business you are in.

STEP 6 – DRIVE VISITORS TO YOUR SITE

Even if your site is all ready to go, it is useless unless you have visitors. I'm consistently amazed by how many website owners still believe that if they build a site, visitors will automatically find it. The adage, "If you build it, they will come," is false when it comes to online business. There are billions of websites so the chance that people will find yours, without a little prompting, is near zero.

The good news is, thanks to free and paid search engine optimization options, there are many ways to put your site in the path of web surfers who are looking for exactly what you sell. Search engines (Yahoo, Google, etc.) are the place most internet users go when they're looking for information. So much so, that the term "just Google it" has become part of our everyday lexicon.

But in order to get listed on a search engine for a particular search term, you need to be able to work with it so they know your business exists. There are a few ways you can do this, which include:

- **Optimize your site with keywords so visitors can find what they are searching for** – using keywords, which are phrases and words that your target audience is typing into search engines, your site can rank highly in the search results for people looking for your product or service. This will make it easier to find your business. In order to make sure you are ranked well, you can embed them in locations on your web pages such as your domain name, title tag, headlines, and image "alt" tags (which are basically word descriptions for your image).
- **Create a network of links that lead search engines to your business** – search engines place emphasis on

the number of links that point to your site from other places on the web. These links can't come from any old site though – they need to be from sites that are considered authorities. It's a bit like networking. The perceived net worth of your business is based on the quality of your networks followed by the quantity of them. Quality comes first.

- **Drive traffic with paid advertising** – you can, of course, use pay-per-click advertising as offered by the different search engines, or else social media advertising such as that offered by Facebook. This requires a bit of capital to do initially – but if done correctly and refined, this can reap quite predictable returns for your business.

I hope this gives you a solid overview of what is involved. As you can see, most of it is based on timeless business principles. Beyond that, it is merely about getting familiar with the context and environment that the internet offers when it comes to business.

9

OPTIONS TRADING

Time – the most precious resource you have. The one that working professionals most need if they are to earn more money, secure a more relaxing lifestyle, and retire with ease.

The problem: how will you find more of it? Simple, you must fully utilize any spare time you have to create more of it. That's exactly why we developed a step-by-step system where you can earn more money in the stock market, no matter what your work commitments might be.

For the past ten years, Mirriam Williams (self-made millionaire and Brand Laureate Award "World's Leading Trading Coach & Trainer"), alongside Wealth Mentors, has helped over 12,000 students around the world earn more money with options trading in as little as 30-minutes per day.

We worked with a single mother with four children who really needed to earn more money to support her family. She wanted to generate a second source of income but had very limited time, as you might imagine. Using options trading and the system we provided her, she was able to support her family using the spare amounts of time she had available.

Similarly, we worked with a lady who decided to start trading when she was seven months pregnant. Eventually, she became a full-time trader and was able to stay at home and be a present mother to her children as they grew up.

When I first wanted to create wealth, I chose options trading because I am a numbers person, and I didn't necessarily love engaging with people face-to-face (until recently). Given the limited time and capital I had due to my work and family commitments, I needed something simple and affordable to get myself started.

Why get involved in trading? Benefits of engaging in options trading include:

- **You can earn money while you sleep**, so you are leveraging your time, rather than trading it for money. One of the most important aspects of successful trading is to be "unconscious" when the market is alive. Rather than sitting in front of a computer, day in and day out, it is better to lock in a trade, shut down your computer, go to sleep, and trust your trade is set up.
- **It can involve as little as 30-minutes** of your time per day, which is invaluable if you are already strapped for time due to work commitments, raising children, and caring for other family members. Most people have a full-time day job. So trading in the evening makes full use of any downtime.
- **It is a low-risk and low-cost venture** to get involved in, provided you are taught the right information and given a step-by-step system to manage risk.
- **Tax benefits** – Many countries in Asia have tax laws that are in favor of the person who invests offshore. For individuals from Singapore, Malaysia, and Hong Kong, any investment income arising from sources

outside that individual's country of tax residence is tax-exempt. With these benefits, not participating in the US market is a huge loss to anyone. The only people who don't feel a loss are those who are not aware of such opportunities! This reminds me of the saying, "Ignorance is bliss!"

- **You can gain confidence without risk.** You don't even have to trade with your own money until you start gaining confidence and consistent results by paper trading: a simulated trade based on real stock market data.

In this chapter, we will cover how we can leverage simple methods to generate high results with minimal effort to radically impact your finances and change your life. First, let us explore what it takes to be a successful trader.

"I am a business owner. I joined Wealth Mentors because the training is so easy. I never traded options before and I am glad with the results. I have turned $5,000 to $11,000 in 7 weeks."
— Thomas Pendi, Indonesia

CHARACTERISTICS OF A SUCCESSFUL TRADER

Unlike most pursuits in life, trading is not an art but rather a science. As such, achieving success through trading requires strong personal discipline with good and consistent habits. It suits people who naturally love routine and process: doing certain things in a particular way, on a regular basis, without constantly trying to reinvent the wheel. Simply put, there isn't much room for creativity and emotional subjectivity in trading because there is a proven system that you must follow to maximize your gain and minimize your pain. It requires one to make methodical, rational, and timely decisions rather than impulsive or intuitive ones. Lastly, time is always of the essence; if you don't execute your decision in a timely manner, the opportunity to participate in a particular trade will pass you by.

"I teach you to always measure the risks before taking on a position. Novice investors shop for returns, while experts size up the risks because they know the returns will come."
– Mirriam MacWilliams

If you believe you exhibit any of the following characteristics, trading might be a great way to start your additional wealth creation ventures:

- Prefer to follow a routine and can commit to simple consistent actions daily.
- Decisiveness for action.
- Ability to gather and interpret information non-emotionally.

If you are a process-driven person who loves certainty and low risk and appreciates analyzing data, then trading is a great way to start. The question now is, where do you start? There are a myriad of financial instruments that you can trade but to shorten your search, we will zoom in on Shares and Options.

SHARES VS OPTIONS

Here's the boring technical part. An option differs from a share in the sense that it is not a value you own in a company. It is, like the term implies, "the right, but not the obligation, to buy or sell shares at a predetermined price and by a predetermined date in the future." The right to buy is called a "Call" option. And the right to sell is called a "Put" option.

In simple terms, owning Options allows you the right to buy

or sell shares, as their value is "derived" from shares (options are part of a larger group of trading securities called "derivatives"). This is also why options only cost a small fraction of the cost of shares.

Also, unlike shares, Options only last for a limited period of time. You choose the date when they "expire" in value. To be clear, you never intend to hold them to that expiry date. Usually, you sell them well before the expiry date. The longer the expiry date, the higher the cost of the option, simply because you can take a longer period to decide on whether you want to exercise your option.

Think about it this way: you go out for a meal at an all-you-can-eat buffet. If the meal goes for 5-hours instead of 2-hours, you have the choice to eat for a much longer time. So the potential value you derive from the option to eat whenever you want (during that time frame) and whatever you want (all you can eat) is higher. Therefore, you would expect that a ticket to the 5-hour all-you-can-eat buffet is going to be more expensive than the 2-hour option (assuming of course, that the food quality is the same).

Traders typically use Options to hedge their portfolio risk and to speculate on the market. Patience, I will teach you how you can strategically use it to do both.

WHY TRADE OPTIONS INSTEAD OF SHARES?

Shares you own can be of benefit if they rise in value, or if they are on the rise after having bottomed out, at which point you could buy them for a relatively cheap price. However, if the stock price drops, you lose money. You make money when stock prices go up.

With options, you can profit regardless of whether the share value goes up, down, or sideways (whereas with shares you only profit when the share value increases). For each stock, there are two types of Options: "Calls" if the indicators show that the stock price is going up, and "Puts" if the indicators show it's going down. You get rewarded either way, so long as you picked the correct option to buy. It is a matter of calculating which direction the stock market is likely to take and how much a stock can move in a particular direction.

For example, if you purchased a $3 Put Option on a $60 stock, you bought the right to sell a stock at $60 dollars within an agreed timeframe. Say a few days later the stock drops $6 in value to $54 dollars, you have essentially gained $6 of value (since you have the right to sell it back to the market at $60). With your investment of $3, you have effectively gained $6 – this means that a 10% movement in the $60 stock has resulted in a 100% profit on your investment!

Also, since Options are a fraction of the cost of shares, you can afford to invest some additional money by buying more Options, but in different stocks in different industries. Therefore, you are able to diversify your portfolio and spread your risk. This will also increase your dollar returns far beyond what you could have earned from shares. In a nutshell, options can help produce large profits at minimal risk, and with low capital expenditure.

"My profits exceed my monthly salary! I work because I choose to."
— **Karen Hong, Marketing Manager**

SURELY THERE IS A DOWNSIDE TO TRADING OPTIONS, RIGHT?

The fact is that around 70% of options traders lose money. Why? Because they don't have the right knowledge, strategy, traits, environment, system, mentorship, and the list goes on... Of course, with the benefit of learning a proven options trading system, your risk can be drastically mitigated. It goes without saying, you must know what the risks are, and then find and apply the techniques to minimize them.

RISK AND REWARD ARE INSEPARABLE

It's about managing it effectively to succeed. There is a time element involved. Options expire within a certain time period, so you are essentially buying time. You need to keep asking yourself, "How much time am I buying? How much time do I have before that Option expires? When do I need to close on my options contracts?" Timing is critical.

There's also a particular amount of volatility associated with Options that will partly determine the potential profit. Volatility is the degree to which the price of a stock fluctuates up and down in a given time frame. The more volatile a stock, the less predictable its movement is. That makes it difficult to take a winning position safely.

Once you understand the key elements associated with Options trading, they can actually be extremely helpful in rapidly making you money. The key to successful trading with minimum risk is to learn a step-by-step, proven trading system, built on a framework of solid money management principles.

You and most people reading this book, probably engage in one of the riskiest activities in the world – driving. However, with practice, procedures, and safety mechanisms, you can manage this risk and get from A to B without too much of a fuss. It just takes guidance and practice. Again, it's all about receiving the right training.

DIFFERENCE BETWEEN AN INVESTOR AND A TRADER

There are two types of individuals within this wealth vehicle: investors and traders.

Investors adopt a "buy and hold" philosophy. They hold positions for a long period of time. This can be weeks, months, or even years.

Traders are different. They wanted to make money yesterday. Traders hold positions for days or weeks and, in some cases, for just a few hours. Investors and traders use many of the same tools and techniques, but they adapt them to their trading personality and time frame.

Investors choose solid, quality stocks because they will hold their positions for longer periods. They use Fundamental Analysis (through the stock's earnings report) to select stocks that have strong fundamental strength with promising long-term outlooks. Investors are not concerned with the daily price fluctuations. They know that they own fundamentally strong companies that, in the long run, should eventually go up in price.

Traders, on the other hand, can choose a style that matches their own personality and risk tolerance. A "day-trader" is one who is in and out of a stock in less than a day and never carries a position overnight. Relatively few traders can function in this stressful environment for very long. Most traders fall into the categories of swing, momentum, or position traders. These individuals usually hold their positions from a few days to a few weeks, depending upon the market.

They let the prices determine entries and exits. The fundamentals are not as important to a trader as they are to an investor: price movement takes precedence. Both investors and traders should monitor their positions on a daily basis. Neither need to spend more than thirty minutes each day tracking and evaluating their portfolios.

Whether you consider yourself a trader or an investor, make sure that you learn how to make good entries and exits. When we teach investors, we emphasize the importance of this discipline. The other discipline for both traders and investors is proper money management. It is impossible to overemphasize the importance of the use of "stop-loss" orders. It is also vital to know your targeted exit point before you enter any trade.

PROTECTING YOUR TRADES AND SPOTTING OPPORTUNITIES

Anyone who invests or trades in any market does so with one goal: to generate a return on that investment capital (to make money). Our approach is to view the US Market as a business—a place to conduct research and implement methods that are designed to generate a profit. Investing or trading in any market utilizes the same principles: buy low, sell high. Even if you are accurate just 50% of the time in your decision to invest or trade, you can still be profitable.

Your primary focus needs to be the preservation of your investment capital. The aim is to protect your capital so you never run out of money, and so that you always have some funds to invest. Firstly, be able to determine your potential profit target and your potential downside. Secondly, you need to know precisely where to exit even before entering the trade such that your investment capital is protected.

THE PRESERVATION OF YOUR CAPITAL IS THE KEY TO A SUCCESSFUL TRADE

As a beginner trader, the temptation is to quickly take a position and start making money right away. However, bringing in no profits at all is still better than losing any part of your capital. It is logical. We must remove human emotion from the equation temporarily, so we can make sound decisions. If you have a tendency to want variety and to express creativity, you might not be naturally suited to trading. Again, it is up to you.

Now consider this – the more you lose in trading, if you

don't execute the proper stop loss, the longer it will take to get back to where you started from – because you have a larger amount to make up and because now you have a smaller investment capital to work with. For example, making 10% on a $10,000 account earns you $1,000; however, if you have lost half of that investment capital and have only $5,000 left, making 10% on your money will earn you only $500. You would have to do that twice to make the same $1,000.

Preserving your investment capital is obvious. However, avoiding loss of profit opportunities is not so obvious. Let's imagine two investors. Mike buys a stock (investor) expecting it to go up and finds that within a specified period of time, it does not. However, he is convinced that it will go up and decides to wait it out. He may end up holding the stock for 2-3 months before selling it at break-even.

Leslie, on the other hand, buys the same stock at the same time as Mike, but once he sees that it is not going up, he sells at a small loss. He buys another stock and makes 30% profit (he learned how to take advantage of leveraging his investment capital in the US market by using options instead of buying the stock this time). His next trade loses 10% but after that, he does two profitable trades: one with a 30% profit and the other with a 50% profit. Because he is growing his account, he makes these percentages on a larger and larger capital basis each time. At the end of the same time period, his account has grown by 100% (30% - 10% + 30% + 50%).

Whose money management decisions turned out to be the best? Can you see how the idea works? You now have your investment capital earning a return for you.

In addition, you clearly do not want to have your entire investment capital in the market at all times. Know that if you are an experienced trader and have an alternative source of income, you can take more aggressive trades compared to a beginner trader. A beginner should focus on more conservative methods in order to build up their investment capital, as well as confidence.

Patience and discipline can go a long way in ensuring your investment capital stays intact so that you can always make a profit another day.

A sound money management principle has two main goals:

1. Avoid losing money.
2. Avoid missing profit opportunities because you may have your investment capital tied up in trades that are going nowhere for a long period of time (or may even be going against you).

THE MAGIC OF PAPER TRADING

The process we recommend after your initial training is to refine your skills by paper trading (virtual trading without money) until you develop the familiarity and confidence to trade with a small sum of real money.

Do the world's greatest athletes practice their skills before they play? Of course! In fact, they usually practice much more than they play. Practice is one of the keys to their success. So it follows that the same should apply to options traders.

Of course, there is a difference in the emotions you feel between paper trading and "live" trading. You need to experience this and become used to it, but just like sports, the pressure of a real contest is always different from the pressure of a practice match for development.

Keep your money safe. Refine your skills first, and then add more money. Once you are confident with paper trading, we recommend starting to trade with a small sum of real money first, even just US$2,000 to start.

Why not more money? Because if you can't make it with

US$2,000 to start, you can't make it with $10,000, $50,000, or $100,000.

SHOULD YOU LISTEN TO MAINSTREAM STOCK MARKET GURUS?

My recommendation is always to put outside influences aside. The average retail investor or trader is rarely going to gain an advantage by following the advice of stock market gurus. The same goes for trying to gain an "edge" in investing by following different news events. They are not designed to give you an edge in your investing. Generally, when information regarding a stock is made public, the market has already reacted. The stock has already made its move either up or down. It is like steering your car while looking in the rearview mirror.

Such was my own personal experience when I began learning how to invest in the US stock market; everyone seemed to have an opinion. But what happens when the information begins to contradict itself? It's really quite immobilizing. Does this mean that you have no means of gaining an advantage in your investing? Not at all. Observe what the "price action" is telling you about a stock. Price action is all the information you need to know about the impending direction in a stock.

It tells you whether your particular stock is being overbought or oversold. When you implement simple methods associated with technical analysis, you can determine with quite a bit of your own accuracy the direction the stock wants to travel. You would now be in a much better position to take confident trades.

OPTION STRATEGY REVEAL – 9 HIGH-PROBABILITY TRADES IN A YEAR

Now that we have all the basics out of the way, let's explore a strategy that has been generating huge profits for my students and me. Bearing in mind all the fundamentals mentioned above, I will now share with you a simple strategy that you can apply right away. I call this the public holiday strategy. Why? Because if you look at the charts and go back in time tracking the 9 U.S. public holidays, you will find that a week or two before the actual holiday itself the markets tend to rally (i.e., go up in price)!

Don't believe me? Check it out for yourself on your respective trading platform(s) to see. Now, I am in no way whatsoever making any guarantees here, but a simple cursory glance at the charts will reveal that this is indeed a phenomenon that occurs rather frequently. The interesting thing is that this isn't based on any fundamental or technical analysis, just pure observation from experience!

Now, if you are feeling confident, go try it out on your demo account (i.e., paper trade) first. Once ready, feel free to trade live. bearing in mind those key nuggets that I have shared above. You will find that this may be the simplest and easiest strategy to come across. What if I told you that 90% of the strategies that Mirriam and I teach are this easy? The hardest part is really to get over your own self-limiting beliefs that trading is difficult so that you can quickly get on board our live webinars and join our community to trade profitably together.

MYTHS

MYTH #1 – Options trading is complicated and hard to understand.

At Wealth Mentors, we don't suggest that Options Trading is

easy; it takes work. Just as a lake looks like its growth and beauty is simple, we also know that every day, at a microscopic and organismic level, life forms are working and persisting to carry out what they are naturally best at. That's what helps the lake to flourish. For instance, many traders teach and follow 30 plus different methods for trading, when accurately executing just one of two proven strategies well is enough to make you wealthy.

Of course, you still need several days of initial education to understand and use Options profitably, but once you get it, it is just a matter of consistent application. Part of having the right skills to make substantial profits from Options trading is to ensure that you have the right environment – people to learn and trade with so that iron can sharpen iron.

FOCUS ON THE FEW THAT FUNCTION AND IGNORE THE MANY THAT DON'T

The simplicity of a proven, easy-to-understand, and profitable system is the key. Our international trading guru Mirriam MacWilliams makes 80% of her profits from less than five methods. Today, she's a self-made multi-millionaire. Attempting to understand a large number of methods can confuse you, consume a lot of your time, or worse yet, make you procrastinate. This is not a helpful trait for trading, which involves efficient use of time and decisive action.

MYTH #2 – Options trading requires you to take a long time to become a technical analyst.

There is a temptation to make stock analysis very complex, and the majority of people who follow such methods wonder why they don't make money. The problem is that they crave perfection, so they seek more complex explanations for why stocks move in particular ways and complicated methods for addressing those complexities. The key thing to understand is that the stock market is *not* perfect.

It has been said that 80% of the reasons why stocks move is due to human psychology and that the human emotions of fear and greed sometimes create irrational movements, especially at the extreme points of market movements. For example, the greed of the dot-com boom in the late 1990s and early 2000s quickly turned to fear in early 2001 with the dot-com bubble bursting.

No trading system is foolproof, but a simple and proven set of techniques will help you to avoid the confusion and delays of complex methods while *minimizing* your risk and *maximizing* your gain.

MYTH #3 – To be a successful trader, you have to trade all night.

Some people in the Asia Pacific region trade 6½ hours each night until at least 4:00 am, sleep for 2 to 3 hours, and then go to their daytime job, after which they go home to sleep for another 2 to 3 hours before the market opens at 9:30 pm. Some quit their daytime jobs in the early stages of their trading even before they are able to generate a consistent flow of trading profits.

We do not recommend this pathway. This is a surefire recipe for disaster in terms of your health, financial security, personal circumstances, and all other areas of your life. It's not a way to gain financial or time freedom. It is entirely contrary to our wealth philosophy.

A lot of the action in the market happens in the first 1½ hours. After which, it often goes quiet because of the US lunchtime. It becomes active again only after about 2:00 am Asia time when most people want to be in bed, which is an advantage for Asia, as you can lock in your trading position, go to sleep, and not be tempted to tamper with your decision.

PLANT THE SEED, NURTURE IT, AND LET IT GROW

Think about a flower. Once you set the seed in good soil, give it water, and make sure it has access to sunlight, it will grow. You simply repeat the action, leave it alone, and let it grow. Rather than dig up the soil to check on the seed and reposition it, you let it be and exercise patience on a well-executed decision.

You want spare time to focus on living your life. Ask yourself, where do you want to be in the middle of the night? I daresay you want a good night's sleep, or you would love to spend some quality time with your partner and family, participating in the things that matter most in life: friends, family, health, and hobbies.

Gladly, we only select trainers who value lifestyle. Mirriam MacWilliams, for example, originally created her trading methods so as to trade only 30 to 90 minutes per day. She mainly wanted time freedom, not wealth. Along the way, she has also found that her practical and balanced approach generates significant profits. Since the mid-1990s, it has made her a multimillionaire. Today, using those methods allows her time with her husband as well as to explore her hobbies, such as scuba diving.

MYTH #4 – It's better to get an expert to trade on your behalf.

The path to true wealth involves taking personal control over your financial situation – getting Wealthy By Choice. I'm not saying you can't leverage your time by engaging experts to help you do certain activities in your life, such as accountants and financial advisors. What I do mean is, take control of your wealth generation activities. This means learning, practicing, and using the skills that can produce significant profits. It means applying the simple and powerful principles of wiring yourself for wealth as we covered in Chapter 3 of this book.

If you decide to hand your money to someone else to trade for you (rather than doing it yourself), the inevitable result is that you become reliant on that other person to create wealth for you. Even if that person has a good track record, what if something happens to them? They are only one person, not an organization, and if they're gone, your journey towards financial freedom comes to a complete stop. It's a single point of failure.

Plus, no one is going to be more committed to your life than you. Rain, snow, or shine. Just like the lake: if you care for it, nurture it, and your livelihood is dependent on it, you are almost guaranteed to get up in the morning and give it what it needs. Who will make sure it is not contaminated and has the best chance of thriving? You will.

MYTH #5 – You need to buy expensive, proprietary software from the options trainer

This is a big myth and one that is costing many people who have unfortunately been sold into this idea when it comes to trading. Some people attract you into their course with a low price, only to offer you some software at the back-end of the course that you must buy if you want to effectively trade using their strategies and techniques.

These pieces of software are sometimes referred to as "black boxes," and some of them are priced at up to $5,000. Some even provide signals as to when to enter and exit a trade, so you don't have to work it out for yourself. So you become dependent on the software and quickly forget why you should be trading at those points. Some also have monthly maintenance fees of around $100 per month.

The key is to learn self-reliant methods, which allow you to trade on your own without the assistance of such software.

A wooden post can support a tree during its early phases of growth, but for it to continue growing into a large tree, the posts must be removed, and it must learn to grow and support itself. We want you to learn to be wealthy your way because then it will be more sustainable. To save you time, you might want to make use of some free or inexpensive stock filtering tools, but that's about all. You have the freedom to choose, not because you have to use any particular software, but because you are in control given the knowledge you have.

SUMMARY OF THE KEY BENEFITS OF OPTIONS

1 – Liquidity

Options (those traded on the US stock market) are a very popular investment and there's always a market to buy from and to sell to. Liquidity is the key because the more often something is traded, the more easily you can convert it to cash, which is ultimately what you want. In a contrasting example, real estate property can't easily be converted to cash. The process is more tiresome and requires administrative procedures and settling of the contract.

2 – Leverage

Options allow you to profit by controlling a large number of shares with a small investment. Remembering that with options, you only pay for the right to buy (Call) or sell (Put) a share, rather than having to own it. The price of an option is how long you hold that right to buy or sell.

. . .

3 – Limited Risk

Options are only a fraction of the cost of the related shares. You know exactly what percentage of the Option's cost you are risking when you buy.

4 – Large Profits

Option prices often move quickly and by large percentages. When properly managed within a solid, proven system, it can be a massive income creator and possibly lead to extraordinary wealth.

BE WEALTHY BY CHOICE, GET WEALTHY YOUR WAY

When I left my 6-figure a year job to come home and trade for a living, I had no idea of the richly rewarding life that would follow. It was one of the best decisions I ever made in my life. Very early on, I realized that to succeed as a full-time trader, I needed to have the utmost time management and self-discipline. So my first recommendation is to determine how much time you are willing to devote to trading in the stock market since that will determine what type of trading personality you will have.

If you choose this wealth vehicle, I highly recommend getting the proper education in trading and/or investing before you begin. I find that individuals who come to my training with some trading/investing knowledge generally do better. I also recommend that students first paper trade – also called "virtual trading" – without any money to simulate as closely as possible the conditions of live trading. Paper trading is a wonderful way of fine-tuning a strategy. It also allows you to see whether a strategy suits your trading personality.

If you are unable to generate returns while paper trading, then the likelihood is a strategy may not be as well understood as you thought and it is time to revisit the strategy and ensure you understand it well enough to paper trade it again. When you see how quickly your trading account grows while on paper, you will be better prepared to become a successful "full-time" trader. No trader should begin trading real money without first experiencing paper trading! So remember...**Earn the Right to Risk – that's the Best Option!**

The Wealth Engines Action Steps

You've finished Part II and have learned about four wealth vehicles that you can use to build wealth your way. Before you move on to Part III, complete the corresponding exercises found in the *Wealth Creation Workbook*. These exercises help you take the initial steps with the wealth vehicle(s) that you are most drawn to. Go now to www.wealthybychoicebook.com/bonus and download your free PDF copy of the *Wealth Creation Workbook.*

PART III

THE PATH TO SUSTAINABLE WEALTH

10

SUSTAINABLE WEALTH

"If you want one year of prosperity, grow seeds.
If you want ten years of prosperity, grow trees.
If you want a lifetime of prosperity, grow your self-worth."
— Chinese proverb

In this chapter, I would like to share with you the three key observations I have made over my years of sustaining wealth. I include these as insights and philosophies that are worth noting, as you grow more and more into your version of wealth. They are ways of perceiving, almost like a new set of glasses that allow you to see more of the world with greater detail.

Again, this is what has worked for me. You can choose to take what is useful and ignore the rest. I'm simply offering you as many different wealth pathways as I can so that you have access to more choices in life. No one thing will work for everybody. Human nature shows us that every person, including you, is unique in location, physicality, time, and space. These variables are best managed by you. So trust your own judgment because only you truly know what is going on in your life. It is you who is empowered to decide what the best course of action is.

OBSERVATION 1: BUILD ON YOUR WINS

The power of starting with one is never to be underestimated. Once I started earning money, using trading as a vehicle, it created a sense of confidence in me. I came to understand that if I persisted long enough to pursue other ways of generating income while living my life, things would be okay. Since building on one success, my income has diversified enough so that I don't need to be dependent on any one source and am thus less exposed to unexpected changes in the marketplace. So as you gain success in one area of wealth, I recommend that while it is great to celebrate and enjoy it, don't sit around too long. Get into action again and apply those same success formulas to other wealth engines so you can create sustainable wealth.

Aside from generating more money and earning interest in the bank, consider increasing your assets. An asset can be property investment. An asset can be expert knowledge or a skill that you can pass on to another person in exchange for money. In business, you can create a license model for your products or services, thus leveraging your time and earning a commission from licensees who are succeeding in their own businesses too. Or what about buying a business that has the potential to generate you some passive income, such as a credible network marketing business?

You could also become a highly paid consultant for corporations, and as part of your reward package, take a fixed percentage of the additional revenue you help a business generate during the time you are with that company. If you are great at what you do, this sort of win-win arrangement is likely to sustain itself long into the future.

WHEN YOU LEARN THE MINDSET FOR WEALTH, YOUR CREATIVE ABILITY TO GENERATE WEALTH INCREASES

This leads me to the next principle of cross-fertilization. When I got started with Wealth Mentors, an additional stream of income for my business was to attract internationally renowned speakers on different topics. In this way, I was able to attract new groups of people with a new set of needs. In online business terms, this meant building a larger list of people with whom I could interact and build relationships. A bit like having multiple lakes all feeding into each other and connected via veins so that water is never scarce and can also be distributed from one lake to another in the event of overflow (or underflow). Instead of building pipes, build a bigger pool. More pipes will drain the lake, but if you build bigger pools, you have more to draw from.

OBSERVATION 2: LIFE IS LIKE A BUSINESS

"Whoever renders service to many puts himself in line for greatness
– great wealth, great return, great satisfaction, great reputation, and great joy."
— Jim Rohn

In my opinion, life is a business, and it helps me to view it this way. You don't have to agree with me, but it's worth trying on for a moment, so I ask you to consider it. As human beings, we are all living life in service to other things and people, in return for what we want to receive; it is an exchange. What exactly do I mean by this?

A small child is in the business of growing up. While figuring out the world, they are finding ways of gaining what they want (enjoyment/pleasure) from the adults around them. Reward and punishment are something children learn. They learn how to do the right things in order to reap rewards and what to avoid so they don't get punished. From an early age, they understand risk management to a degree, even though they would never call it that. Of course, some children get creative and naughty by bending the rules to their favor, but the point is they are in the business of getting what they want.

A mother is in the business of raising a child. She learns how to gain the resources and knowledge she needs in order to nourish and nurture a child, and at the same time adopts new skills in order to see that through. Effective mothers have to be great at time management, stress management, negotiation, emotional intelligence, and "customer" relations, to name just a few. All of which are priceless traits to have in a business. In return for all these skills, she receives the love of a child and the intangible gifts that come with motherhood.

Even now, as an adult, my life is like a business. I have friends, colleagues, and customers whom I treat favorably because I know that they will return the favor for my sincere deeds. We are all in relationships where a mutual exchange occurs. Even if it isn't monetary, there is something we stand to gain from those relationships. For myself, a lot of the time it is the feel-good experience or the fulfillment, so even though my heart might give to them unconditionally, I still do it because in return I get to feel good. I get to sleep well at night. I get to experience my deeper soul expand to a larger level.

WE ARE ALL EXCHANGING VALUE

If you begin to do this exchange consciously, your world and the world around you become very interesting. Imagine what it would be like if everyone in your neighborhood was specifically looking, on a daily basis, to provide value in exchange for the life they want?

I remember being at an event and asking my customers how many people came to the event because they saw my email invite. I was greatly surprised to see that 50% of people raised their hands. Correction, I was touched because this meant that they have trust in me. I know that this trust didn't come easily. It came from my devotion to delivering them consistent value in the past.

In business, I focus on long-term relationships with my clients instead of "hit and run" short-term gain.

So remember, if you solve people's problems or even just make a positive difference in someone's day, that is your value-add in life. You are literally accumulating customers by looking at what you can give to another. If you can see life as an exchange between human beings, who all possess different gifts, and who all have different needs, you will be amazed at what opportunities show up. You will also be amazed at how this type of thinking makes you feel rich from the inside out.

Today, when I'm taking a retreat or traveling, I am directly incorporating these into my business because I travel to attend events and meet people who will potentially be a part of my business. By seeing my life as a business, I get to align and support different aspects of my personal life too. In my family, my brother cares for the finances in Wealth Mentors, and my sister helps take care of some of the operations. Family and wealth creation are both important to me, so I have found ways to serve both aspects using my business. Today, when my mother comes to my KL office, she feels like she is part of the business as well. She always expresses interest by asking, "How is that Smart Traders program going?" or checking in to ask me how other members of the team are doing. Bringing in that caring and family element to a business really makes it a special place to be.

OBSERVATION 3: TRUST YOUR INTUITION

Sometimes you have to go beyond logic to get results. I learned this the hard way after a particular event in my life. I learned not to go for business deals that sounded good but felt sour. Without mentioning names, I remember being introduced to a various number of investment deals, which were so-called "sure wins." On paper, they even aligned with my values because they could help a lot of people and were financially viable. I thought the deal was too good to be true. So I threw up objections, and of course, a trained salesperson was able to address them one by one very convincingly. But it doesn't stop there. Because I am a facts kind of person, I even contacted all my networks to ask for their opinion, and they thought it was a sound proposal too.

However, something didn't sit right in my stomach or my heart. I felt exhausted by the proposal, rather than energized. But I ignored the feeling, and it really cost me. I remember my wife Tracy saying that "the deal is off" – but I didn't listen.

So the moral of the story is:

1. Listen to your wife (if you have one)
2. Trust your intuition

This intuition can be developed as you meditate more. Meditation and proper breathing can calm your mind, help you become centered, and make clear (intuitive) decision-making easier.

THE JOURNEY CONTINUES

As you might have guessed – my journey of wealth creation continues. It is always about the journey, never the destination. What worked for wealth ten years ago might not be working now strategy-wise. In my business ten years ago:

- I could run ads in the paper and get people to a paid event, and people would sign up. But now, those events are free, or else people won't show up.
- Speakers from the US used to have celebrity status and generate a lot of interest that way. But the market became saturated with them and the results they got didn't match the hype. What attracts people now is genuine experts with new, results-based content.
- My customers used to be focused heavily on financial wealth and quick results. Now, their interests are extended to holistic and timeless wealth that also includes health, wellness, and personal fulfillment.
- The market today is far more focused on social media for the purposes of directly engaging people and building rapport. People hardly read the newspaper, unless they are of a certain generation, and those who do are now supplementing that with the use of online platforms. So, over the years I have had to shift my activities and focus to the online space more and more, to continue to build and sustain the relationships I have with my customers.

With all these changes in wealth strategies, it is the mindset of continual learning and development that will see you through.

What is timeless is your ability to learn to adapt to what is happening, so that what you are producing doesn't ever become out of date. That is the key to sustainable wealth. Just as the lake adapts with the change of season, every activity you have must be adaptable too. Even today, I still invest a lot of money in coaching and mentoring to guide and help me sustain my business. I look at what is happening in the market, and I continually invest time and money to learn more. I always make sure that anyone I learn from has gone through the process themselves and achieved results!

Some knowledge they share might not be new to me, but it never hurts to revisit certain principles. As Jim Rohn once said, "It is not that the information is different, but because you change as a person, how you see that information is different – which can take on an entirely new and profound meaning for your life."

11

HEALTH IS WEALTH

"The first wealth is health."
— Ralph Waldo Emerson

In this final chapter, we focus on wealth beyond the monetary definition. I want to talk about the importance of health and the value of time, which are the most important assets that we have. Have you wondered what it really means to be wealthy? What are the things that matter most should we lose everything today?

CARING FOR YOU

Health as the first wealth is one of the most important principles you will ever learn. Now you might be wondering, "Aaron, how is this going to make me money?" You will be surprised how important health is when it comes to wealth-building and longevity. It is also one of the most overlooked aspects of wealth creation today.

When people have excuses about why they can't create the life they want, you often hear things like:

- "I just don't have the time"
- "I'm too tired"
- "I can't think properly"

All of the above objections have one thing in common – energy. More accurately, the lack of it. Without the right amount of energy, it clearly doesn't matter whether you have all the time in the world or the strategies to build wealth because you won't be able to use it.

However, if you take care of your health, you can increase your energy levels and mental efficiency and make proper use of your time. With the right knowledge, it's really quite simple. The problem is that there is so much misinformation and over-complication in the world of health that it can be really hard to know where to start. Not anymore; in this chapter, you will learn timeless principles that you can apply immediately.

WHY IS BEING HEALTHY SO IMPORTANT TO ME?

My younger brother passed away in August 2020 before his 59th birthday. He had always planned to retire by age 60, but instead, he left behind two young twins and a loving wife. He died due to a nagging back pain that he ignored for the longest time until one day it became unbearable. He finally went to have it checked at the doctors. After some X-rays and reports, the doctor told him that he needed surgery. Although we were reluctant in choosing surgery, the doctor gave assurance that none of his past patients had any issues, and his success rate was 100%. In fact, just a day or two before his operation, another patient of the doctor that sat next to my brother in the waiting area shared with him that her condition had improved tremendously because of a recent surgery done by this same doctor, and that gave my brother confidence.

After the surgery my brother was fine, but he died one month later. Even though my family and I gave our support to him because ultimately it was his choice to proceed or not, deep in our hearts we knew that it was because of the failed surgery that my brother lost his life. At that point, it was not retribution by legal means that came to mind, more so the memory of how I tried to help him and what I could have done better.

I realized my brother's health issues ten years before his untimely death. At least five years before he died, sensing his unhealthy lifestyle, I invited him to a week-long health retreat in Bali to detox and rejuvenate his health. He was feeling very good after the five days, and he could have continued on a plant-based diet after that, but he did not.

The moment he got back home, he reverted to his normal lifestyle and eating habits, proving that learning new things is not the end. You need the right environment to support your growth and continuity of good habits.

Deep down I asked myself, could I have done more for my brother to save him? Although staying healthy is a personal choice, as a brother, I wondered if the results would have been different if there had been a health intervention when he had the opportunity to do so years ago.

"Good health is not something we can buy.
However, it can be an extremely valuable savings account."
— Anne Wilson Schaef

MORE QUALITY ENERGY = MORE TIME FREEDOM

Remember, it's about putting yourself in the position to best make use of the limited time you have to earn more money and create the life you want.

How often do you hear people spending lots of money on medical bills and hospital bills because their health is failing? Suppose you work a job at an hourly rate or run a business, and you get sick often. How would that affect your productivity and income earning potential?

To give you some perspective, absenteeism due to illness, the cost of worker's compensation, and general poor health costs the US economy more than half a trillion dollars a year! According to a new study by The Integrated Benefits Institute, which represents major US employers and businesses, bad health costs $576 billion a year.[1] Of that amount, about $227 billion is from "lost productivity" from employee absenteeism, or what researchers called "presentee-ism," when employees report to work but illness keeps them from *performing at their best*. It's simple, if you aren't performing at your best, not only does your workplace lose money, you do too. Being ill means you lose the energy and time to be productive, in this case, to build wealth. Worse yet, medication and treatment, in more severe cases, costs you money.

It's a fact: not having good health is costly. Therefore, there must be a financial gain in getting your health back on track. Money lost can always be regained; however, with health, there comes a point of no return. You don't need special talent or skill to be healthy; you just need access to the right knowledge and principles to be able to practice it and reap the benefits.

So in this chapter, I am going to share a few principles that can be very simply applied for benefits to show immediately. These were learned and adapted from our health and life transformation guru Skip Archimedes. If you don't recall, Skip was told that he was going to be in a wheelchair for the rest of his life after an accident. Instead, he ended up winning his second British Gymnastics title after being given such a dreadful prognosis.

Today, Skip earns a great living by sharing his wisdom and

insights after having learned from some of the greatest healers of our time. By getting his mind and body aligned for healing, not only did he recover physically, but he also positioned himself to accumulate wealth.

> *"I had suffered since childhood from all manner of ailments, such as asthma, eczema, and many allergies. In my teens, I caught every bug doing the rounds even though I was very fit through swimming and gymnastics training. I decided to try some of the healing methods on myself, and I am now completely free from all of them. I started waking up each morning wanting to get on with life and living it to extremes, and I still do."*
>
> **— Skip Archimedes**

But here's the thing, he didn't learn any "miracle" cures or "mystical" solutions. He learned simple and natural techniques to manage and nurture his body's systems. He was then able to give his body the conditions and nutrition it needed to heal itself, and he combined this with a disciplined mind. Remember, the brain is a muscle too, so you can't possibly have holistic health unless your mind is taken care of. That is exactly why we focused on the power of your mind earlier.

Plus, even if you don't use any of the other wealth-building engines that are directly income-generating, you are likely to perform better at whatever you are doing for a living. That change in performance alone will position you to potentially be paid more for the value you deliver. You will also have the energy to spend time with your children, or at least be present for your friends and family when you have those spare moments. The effect of health on your quality of life has an unbelievable domino effect!

PREVENTION MEASURES AND PRESERVATION

Up to the age of 34, I was always into exercise and didn't have any major health challenges in my life. From 34 onward, I have been eating a plant-based vegetarian diet with no alcohol consumption and no smoking.

Rather than being reactive, I was responsive to the signals at an early age. I found a purpose and embraced teachings and disciplines that helped me keep my mind, body, and spirit on track. So now at age 60, I look at my other friends who struggle with mobility problems, hair loss, and rapidly reducing energy levels, and I say, "Thank goodness I invested in my health!" I am fortunate enough to retain my black hair and many of my friends say, "Wow! You seem to be getting younger!"

Today, I feel younger and even more aligned in purpose with the way I live. The true wealth philosophy includes taking care of my health, and because of that, I have to be a symbol for what I teach.

To give you another example, a student of ours, Darren, joined Skip's Bali Retreat to regain his health. At the time, he weighed 113kg (249 lbs.). Since attending the retreat, he has dropped down to 98kg (216 lbs.), is eating much more healthily, has increased energy, and is vastly more confident in his ability to reach a goal. With his newfound energy, he also attended the Smart Traders Program and built on it by attending Joel Bauer's Profit Point event, securing a land deal worth over $150 million. The new energy he found within himself through Skip's health retreat really got him in the zone to generate wealth more smoothly.

HEALTH AND WEALTH ARE INSEPARABLE

If you create a "why" and get clear on your purpose, your body will be fine.

Health and Wealth can sometimes be like two human legs – both have to be in sync and functional for you to walk forward. I am now at the point where I can feel the energy in my body, especially the difference between say "Char Kuay Tiew" (Singapore famous fried yellow noodles) and a healthy vegetable and fruit juice. So, let's get started with some useful principles for health that I've learned from Skip Archimedes.[2]

This is not an exhaustive list. Rather, I have selected ones that have made a huge difference in my life and are also simple enough for you to implement straight away to start experiencing the benefits within a short period of time.

PRINCIPLE 1 – OXYGENATE WITH CORRECT EXERCISE

Did you know that 90% of our energy comes from oxygen and only 10% from food and water? The three rules of basic survival are:

1. You can live without food for 3 weeks.
2. You can live without water for 3 days.
3. You can live without oxygen for 3 minutes.

So, you can see why it is so important to get enough oxygen in your day. This principle is so simple that it is often overlooked.

With a good supply of oxygen, every single cell in our bodies can stay healthy and regenerate properly. What's even more exciting about a generous intake of oxygen is that you can feed your cells with a vital form of energy that is basically free and contains no calories.

OXYGEN IS AN ABUNDANT RESOURCE FOR HEALTH

I don't mean that you need to get an oxygen tank and breathe through it. This principle is about oxygenating sufficiently via natural forms of exercise that include movement of the body and breathing techniques.

Generally speaking, a good breathing technique is diaphragmatic breathing. This is where you expand your belly (diaphragm) as you breathe in and then contract it as you breathe out. Babies naturally do this, and you were once a baby too. It is about remembering it!

Benefits of Breathing Properly:

- **Using the full capacity of your lungs** in order to bring more oxygen into the body and allow the body to function well.
- **Reducing the toxins and body wastes** from within your body to prevent diseases.
- **Improving your digestion** with the proper way of breathing. Your metabolism and health will start to improve.
- **Developing more concentration and focus** so you can be more effective in your wealth-building activities.
- **Reduced stress levels** and increased relaxation within your mind and body, so you experience serenity and peace of mind.
- **Increased emotional stability** by staying calm even though you may want to express your temper or react negatively to events and people surrounding you. This results in saved energy and allows you to stay focused on the activities most important to you: building and living the lifestyle you want. The one you deserve.

EXERCISE – HOW TO START BREATHING PROPERLY

Each of the following exercises should take 2-3 minutes to complete.

Practice breathing in and out of your nose. Exhaling through the mouth is okay for quick relaxation, but for normal breathing, in and out of the nose is best. Take long breaths but do not force it. You shouldn't hear your breath coming in or out. You're drawing slow breaths, not gulping it or blowing it out. Feel the rhythm of your breathing.

Good breathing is done through the lower torso, rather than the upper torso. Each breath should expand your belly, lower back, and ribs. Relax your shoulders and try not to breathe with your chest. Put your hands on your stomach and feel it rise and fall. If it's not working, push down gently with your hands for a few breaths and let go. Your stomach should start to move more freely. Relax your forehead, face, neck, cheeks, jaw, temples, even your tongue.

Feel the good air entering your lungs and feel the stale air leaving your body. "In with the good, out with the bad" is definitely true here. Make your exhale at least as long as your inhale to make sure all the bad air is gone. Remember, long slow breaths. Most people take 12-16 breaths per minute. Ideally, it should be 8-10. Next, try to make your exhale a little longer than your inhale for a while. Pause after your exhale without taking a breath. Focus on the stillness and on not forcing an inhale. Your body will breathe when it needs to.

EXERCISE – GET SOME PHYSICAL EXERCISE

Once you get the hang of breathing properly in a state of rest, work on your breath control while you are working out. Remember, regular workouts are absolutely necessary for your better health. If you breathe correctly during your workouts, you will maximize the benefits tenfold.

Here are a few tips you can use to exercise effectively. All of them are simple, and you can choose the ones that best fit into your unique lifestyle.

- **Get slightly out of breath** three times a day.
- **Always warm up and stretch your muscles and joints before exercising**. You are going to extend yourself in a way that you haven't done all day, so you need to prepare your muscles, joints, and tendons for the different loads you are about to place on them. You wouldn't drive your car off at full speed without getting it warm first if you want it to last!
- **Start gently** and build up gradually.
- **Never train through pain**. Don't ignore pain. Listen to your body because it may be telling you to temporarily STOP before any further damage is done!
- **Never, ever exercise when you have a bad cold**. One of the few dangerous aspects of exercise is the possibility that a cold or flu virus can damage the heart if intense exercise is taken when the virus is still present. If you are feverish, stay on the sidelines.
- **Exercise should always be fun**. Don't push yourself to exhaustion; enjoy it. The right level will leave you breathless, not speechless.
- **Exercise with other people** occasionally, as this can make it an activity to look forward to while giving you the opportunity to reconnect with someone close to you.
- **Vary what you do daily**. Try to fit some exercise into your daily routine, maybe use the stairs instead of elevators. For short trips, leave the car at home. Try

walking briskly instead. You'll raise your heart rate and get your blood flowing.

- **And last of all – Persist!** It will be worth it in the end. For myself, I jog around the park near my apartment, and there are stairs and ramps so it keeps me active and gets my blood pumping. Then, when I sit on a bench to relax and to hydrate with some water, new ideas or insights reveal themselves to me, and they all help me build my wealth and improve my business.

A HEALTHY BODY IS A HEALTHY MIND

Physical activity can offset age-related disease and decline, so don't just read this; implement these gifts into your lifestyle so you actually feel the benefits. It may have taken you years to get out of shape. By taking things gradually, you will begin to get fitter after just a week or two. Try too hard, and you will risk pushing one of those out-of-shape muscles or joints just too far.

"Inch by inch, life's a cinch. Yard by yard, life's hard."
— John Bytheway

PRINCIPLE 2 – HYDRATE WITH CLEAN WATER

Approximately 70% of the planet is water and approximately 70% of you is made up of water, so it's pretty logical to say that 70% of your intake should be water. This includes water-rich foods as well as actually drinking water.

As your body is made up of mostly water, you can imagine why it is so important to hydrate. If you are thirsty or wait until you are thirsty before you start drinking water, it's too late. You are already dehydrated. Dehydration can impact not only your body physically but your ability to process information and make effective decisions.

HYDRATING IS LIKE GIVING YOURSELF A SHOWER FROM WITHIN

So please understand the value of clean water and keep yourself topped up at all times.

Here are a few facts that I've learned from transformation coach Skip Archimedes:

- The biggest trigger of tiredness during the day is a lack of water.
- If your body water drops only 2%, you can experience short-term memory loss, trouble with basic mathematical calculations (which is important if you want to earn more money and build wealth!), and difficulty focusing on the computer screen or on a printed page.

On the plus side, if you do hydrate properly:

- Even slight dehydration can slow down your metabolic rate by as much as 3%. So if you are looking to lose fat (and most of us probably need to shed a few pounds), then it's best to boost your metabolism with water.
- One glass of water gets rid of hunger pangs for most people.
- The normal amount of 8-10 glasses of water a day can drastically reduce back and joint pain for most people who suffer from it.
- Drinking 5 glasses of water daily decreases the risk of colon cancer by 45%, breast cancer by 79%, and bladder cancer by 50%. Wow! That's not even the recommended daily intake of 8-10 glasses! So the more you drink, the longer you live.

Of course, like anything, there is always a balance. You must not over-hydrate because that can have adverse effects too, but hydrating isn't something that is complicated. You just may not have been clear before on the full range of benefits that adequate hydration can give you in all areas of your life! Now that you do know, all you need to do is implement it.

"The first thing anyone can do about any issue is get informed."
— Adora Svitak

To make sure you are getting enough water – and pardon the vulgarity – you can examine the toilet after you pee. Make sure your pee is clear, not yellow. Drinking plenty of water will help remove unwanted toxins from your body and prevent the many health conditions and health problems caused by dehydration.

Best yet, it's simple to do! Either grab some mineral water or apply a filter system to your tap, bottle up, and voila!

EXERCISE – HYDRATION

Try drinking two liters of water a day (more if you exercise regularly). Do this daily for three months. It takes about that much time for your blood to recycle. A simple way of doing it daily is this:

1. Buy 2 one-liter glass bottles.
2. Fill them up with mineral, spring, or filtered water.
3. Make sure you finish them both over the course of a day (not all at once!) before you go to sleep.

PRINCIPLE 3 – SUPPLEMENT WITH ESSENTIAL VITAMINS AND MINERALS

Vitamins and minerals are essential to life. Without them, we couldn't think, breathe, digest food, or even walk. Like anything in health, things work holistically. It's either you have everything you need in balance or something is missing and your health is failing in some area.

You must supplement your diet with many essential vitamins and minerals. I understand you might be trying to rely on eating real food. Unfortunately, in this day and age, much of the soil is depleted, our vegetables and fruit bear fewer nutrients and more sugar, the air is polluted, processed food has become the norm, and less sunlight is hitting the earth. All these factors mean that we need to absorb more supplemental vitamins and minerals than ever before in order to keep our bodies functioning optimally.

Worse yet, the average person is awake and working way after sunset, whereas traditionally, people didn't stay up that late because of the lack of electricity. As a result, they had much more sleep during which to recover. So, the traditional way of eating for nutrition fails to fulfill the additional needs of modern-day living.

With all the health hazards on our planet, survival of the fittest is the name of the game. The best way to become the fittest is to arm your body with proper nutrition. The best way I have found to avoid problems associated with poor nutrition is to use a proper supplement. I am not saying that health supplements should replace a healthy diet, but you need a supplement to complement your diet to make sure that you get enough of the essential vitamins and minerals every day.

SUPPLEMENT DOES NOT MEAN REPLACEMENT

Natural is always best when it comes to supplements. This means that your supplement must be free from dyes, allergens, or artificial preservatives, fillers, bulking agents, and other harmful chemicals. However, the naked truth here is revealed once again. What do I mean? Petrol and coal derivatives can be used as the glue that holds the tablet together. Because this comes directly from the earth they can put 'natural' on the label; shocking! If in doubt, Google the words you don't understand on the label, but be prepared to be shocked, as you'll probably find out you've been swallowing a petrol or coal derivative. Additives are frequently present in many common brands too.

While it's virtually impossible to avoid allergens, you must take extra care to choose products where they are minimal. Minerals and other trace nutrients are also necessary to maintain our general health and to give our bodies the tools they need to fight off health problems. Vitamins also require the presence of these minerals to function correctly in the body, so unless it contains all these nutrients, any vitamin supplement you take will be useless. In short: supplements are necessary because our food options are so depleted.

Thinking of putting it off? I'll share with you a story of a colleague I had when working in the corporate world. Every day, she would complain to me that she found it hard to focus or that she was dizzy. When she got a blood test, she found out she was deficient in a few minerals, and in particular, iron. It was recommended to her to supplement her diet with iron, but she kept putting it off. She said she was always too tired after work to remember or bother going to a health shop to buy the supplement. That procrastination came at a cost. She ended up working *longer* hours at work, making *silly* mistakes on projects, and sacrificing *quality time* with her partner.

The point is, sitting around, waiting, and saying, "I'll do it later" isn't going to help. Act now so you can act more in the future. Choose to have the energy and vitality to pursue a life of wealth – a life worth living.

PRINCIPLE 4 – EAT FOR NUTRITION

This is about fueling your body. Healthy eating is not about fad diets, strict nutrition plans, having "cheat days," being painfully thin, or starving your body of the foods you crave.

Instead, it is about adopting a lifestyle in which you ensure that you fuel your body with the nutrients it needs to give you loads of stored energy so that you can feel great doing the things you love. Many of today's most prevalent and lethal diseases are a direct result of what we eat. In fact, many of them were unknown until the advent of processed foods early in the last century. It's no surprise that these same diseases are virtually unknown in truly undeveloped parts of the world, where the staple diet is still based on naturally occurring, often wild, foods.

As a benchmark, your body should be slightly more alkaline than acidic. An acidic body leaves you open to infection and disease. Without exception, processed foods turn your body acidic. So it's not just the fast foods, fizzy drinks, sweets, and cakes that are to blame. Just about anything in a packet is conspiring to send you into the hands of a doctor. To achieve greater immunity and improved health, you should stop eating processed, refined foods and start eating whole, unprocessed, fresh-as-possible raw vegetables, fruits, beans, grains, nuts, seeds, and lots of pure, clean water.

Research is conducted and published every day to show the miraculous functions of nutritious foods.[3] However, the best place to start is to change your eating patterns at your own pace. A person who has been eating a high-fat, fast-food diet for their whole life cannot expect to embrace a plant-based diet overnight. The body and mind need time to adjust to the healthy lifestyle you want to adopt. After all, you will be more successful at sticking with it for life if you go into it slowly.

SMALL CHANGES ARE MORE SUSTAINABLE

You can start reducing the amount of processed foods and start crowding them out by introducing more whole foods and fresh produce. As you do this, you will not only notice an increase in your energy levels, but you will also start to decrease your cravings for processed foods as well as decreasing the amount you have to eat to feel fed! That means you could potentially save a good amount of money on your grocery shopping, which can then be reinvested in other money-making and wealth creation activities. That's exactly what I mean when I say by caring for your health, you are creating more opportunities for wealth.

PRINCIPLE 5 – GET SOME SUN

Once upon a time, the sun was prescribed as a general tonic to heal almost any ailment known to man, since it provides the foundation of energy for all life on earth. Sun exposure, in moderation, is downright necessary for our health and well-being. The main reason is that vitamin D, the sunshine vitamin, can prevent certain cancers, diabetes, heart disease, osteoporosis, and some autoimmune diseases.

Vitamin D isn't called "the sunshine vitamin" for no reason. Yes, sunshine is a good thing when taken in moderation. Vitamin D is produced by your skin in response to exposure to ultraviolet radiation from natural sunlight. An appropriate amount of exposure each day is all it takes to help prevent numerous diseases. When we go outside and expose at least 40% of our skin to the sunlight without sunscreen for about 10 to 15 minutes every day, we can be sure that our bodies are making the recommended amount of "sunny D."

(*Note:* Absorption rates can vary depending on skin, color, weight and other factors)

You may be wondering, "Well, won't I get more vitamin D if I stay in the sun for as long as possible?" Nope. Photosynthesized Vitamin D will not be stored by the body once the optimum level has been reached, so there is no benefit from deliberately staying out in the sun for longer.

UV exposure is cumulative. Your skin never forgets. Never sunburn. Should you become

pink, do not increase the time in the sun for several days.

PRINCIPLE 6 – REST AND RECOVER

Rest for the short term and sleep for the long haul. We've all heard that we need at least eight hours of sleep every night, but recent surveys show that more people are actually sleeping less than six hours every night.[4] A couple of hours of lost sleep here and there might not sound so bad, but when you consider that if you lose two hours every day, that's 14 hours that you lose per week (or approximately two full nights of sleep).

With so many demands on our time, we may not stop to consider the effects of not getting enough rest. The fact is that chronic sleep loss can contribute to health problems such as weight gain, high blood pressure, depression, and a deteriorating immune system.[5] Rest is a time of repair and renewal. It does most of the jobs that sleep does but at a lower level, while we are wide awake.

If you don't drink some water before you feel thirsty, you are on the way to being dehydrated. In the same way, if you don't rest before you become over-tired, you become a danger to yourself. Whether your exhaustion is mental or physical, you become less efficient the longer you go without rest.

Sleep is the brain's prescription for complete recovery from all the damage done in the course of a busy day. Specific benefits of sleep:

- It restores the body's energy supplies that have been depleted through the day's activities.
- Muscle tissue is rebuilt and restored.
- It's a time for restoring mental energy and specifically helps in consolidating memory.
- Assists in keeping metabolism and weight at normal levels.
- Assists with keeping the immune system functioning well.

Serious sleep disorders have been linked to hypertension, increased stress hormone levels, and irregular heartbeat. All of your healthy eating, exercising, and avoiding caffeine won't do your heart any good if you aren't getting enough sleep!

PRINCIPLE 7 – BE MINDFUL AND MEDITATE

Since 1994, I have embraced the mentorship and guidance of my spiritual master, Supreme Master Ching Hai, and my learning from her continues. She teaches primarily the Quan Yin Meditation method, where we use light and sound to enhance the depth of our meditation.

More importantly, for the last twenty-seven years, I have been joining meditation groups in Singapore once or twice a week, and minimally twice a month in a place in Geylang. It has been crucial for my journey that I have the right level of accountability so I do not get distracted and can stay on track. The key here is that we cannot do it alone; our environment is stronger than our willpower.

YOUR DAILY DEVELOPMENT PLAN

Now that you have wired yourself from the inside out (mind *and* body), it is time to choose the right wealth vehicle that will suit you in terms of:

1. Your natural gifts and talents, and
2. The life you want to create for yourself, and the purpose you want to serve.

Once you have a wealth vehicle, you can look at your life as a whole, and create and execute a daily development plan.

For myself, a typical daily plan looks like this:

1. **I meditate** in the morning from anywhere between 10-minutes to 1 hour or otherwise attend a meditation session one to two times a week in Singapore. This keeps my mental and emotional health in check.
2. **I exercise** for 45-minutes, five times a week to keep my physical health together.
3. **I take daily walks** near the local lake to ease my mind and prepare myself for the day.
4. **I manage and work with my team** in my business from 1 pm – 6 pm, Monday to Friday. Business is an important vehicle for me to serve my purpose, which is to help people just like you earn more money and live the life they want. I want to spread the possibility that everyone can thrive in abundance if they apply themselves to it.
5. **I look at my trading** from Monday to Friday, between 10:30 pm and 11:00 pm. This is great for me because I like exercising my brain, and I like wealth vehicles that involve limited time input.

6. **I spend time with my wife and daughter** and plan trips for the year well in advance.
7. **I attend all my speakers' training sessions** to sharpen my skills so that I can continually serve my customers and clients.

In this way, I take care of my health, business/purpose, family, and finances. This is the life I live and it is the life I love! Yours might be different, but the important thing is that you start planning what will get you closer to your goals and begin living in accordance with that plan to the best of your ability.

12

A DEEPER PURPOSE

"My mission in life is not merely to survive, but to thrive; and to do so with some passion, some compassion, some humor, and some style."
— **Maya Angelou**

Your purpose in life is not to make money. Your purpose encompasses much more than being a responsible parent, an ethical employer, or a valuable member of society, though they may form a critical component of your purpose. Your life's purpose will become clear when you understand who you are and what kind of experience you were meant to have on this Earth.

PURPOSE IS DEVOTING YOURSELF TO THAT ONE THING YOU ARE BRINGING TO THIS PLANET

It's that thing you can't stop thinking about or talking about, it's on your mind 24/7, and without it you would feel at a loss. It is this direction that will give your life reason.

When you are living your passion, you are filling your life with the things that make you smile. Having a totally directed mind and a purpose that is strong will help you wake up every morning inspired and ready to live your day with a smile on your face. Finding your purpose requires a high degree of self-inquiry. The threads of your life reveal the purpose of your life, and it has been with you all along. Here is a simple question that will help you uncover a part of your purpose: What did you always dream of becoming as a child?

Just imagine yourself as innocent as you were as a child, as naïve to the corruption and pain that you can see now that you are an adult. What was it that you wanted to accomplish? Write that down. Is that what you still want to achieve or at least part of what you still desire? Keep brainstorming your list. It may take you some time and many attempts to reach a form of words that you are comfortable and excited about adopting and nurturing as your true purpose. Keep at it!

Persevere because the answer you finally come to will sustain you for a long time to come.

BE IN THE MOMENT

Although we plan for the future, it's important to live for the moment. I want to share with you another story that has impacted me deeply from this book *Chasing Daylight,* written by Eugene O'Kelly. Although this story has a tragic ending, there are many poignant lessons to be learned.

Eugene O'Kelly was the top-notch CEO and Chairman of KPMG in the US. At the age of 53, during the height of his career, his doctor told him that he had incurable brain cancer and had only 3 to 6 months left to live. Some people, upon hearing such news, would not accept it, but he did. O'Kelly accepted his fate. Instead of spending time to find a cure, he decided to invest his little remaining time in the best possible way.

Being a rich, powerful, privileged man from one of the largest accounting firms, Eugene had been very busy his entire life running his business and being good at his job. His days were filled with executive meetings, but suddenly, his appointment became something very different.

This announcement caught him unprepared because despite having everything, he had no time to catch up with friends and do the things that would make him happy or enjoy life. Instead of seeking a cure, he wrote a book about it. He wanted to know the meaning of life, and the little pleasures that he had missed – which are the big things actually. Ironically, the first and maybe the last lesson that he needed to learn was to slow down, as his life was always busy.

With only 100 days left to live, he decided to slow down and dedicate the remaining days to re-examine his life. This was especially hard for him because, for the last twenty-five years, his life was driven by 1 to 2-year plans and was always on the go. However, once he made the decision to slow down, he realized that there were four things that were the most important to him.

One is nature and the environment around him that he had not appreciated for so long. Second was his family. Third was his friends, and the fourth was living in the moment. All four of these things felt alien to O'Kelly because, for the longest time, all he could think and focus on was the growth of his company. During his final days, he finally stopped thinking about distant plans...not months ahead, weeks ahead, days ahead, or even hours ahead. All he thought about was what his next 60 seconds would look like. That was being in the moment.

He realized that he needed to quickly pivot and embrace a new lifestyle, from his rich and powerful lifestyle with back-to-back meetings to a slower pace of doing things in order to reflect on his life's journey and pen down his final thoughts in his book. I would like to share with you some of the lessons from O'Kelly that I have found to be most meaningful.

For the first 25 years of his working life, when he was still healthy, Eugene didn't realize there were many important things that went unnoticed. For example, the garden is beautiful and nature is nice. And every bite of the sandwich is delicious.

Those are the fleeting moments of life, which were inaccessible to him, because he was always busy, chasing things non-stop. If only he could have paused and meditated, to steal a minute away from his busy routine – that would have made a difference.

RELATIONSHIPS MATTER

Value relationships with people who matter most to us – not keeping them at a distance, or only meeting up with them once in a while when we are FREE.

In deciding on the best way to say goodbye to his loved ones, he created a system where he drew a small, medium, and big circle on top of each other. The innermost circle represented his family, the outer circle represented his friends, the outermost circle represented his associates and others who impacted his life. After populating the names, he realized that the number of people he wanted to bid goodbye to as closure was a thousand. He pondered on how he should go about this – inside to out or outside to in? O'Kelly chose the latter and began saying goodbye to those on the outermost circle first while working his way towards his family. As such, he started to contact each and every one of his contacts one by one.

On each private phone call, O'Kelly would recall in detail how they met and enjoyed their time together, rekindle fond memories of what made them become friends, and express his deep gratitude for the things that he learned from them as well as the exact qualities that he appreciated about his friends. His friends were so warmed by his kind and thoughtful gesture. O'Kelly took the opportunity to invite his friends to his residence to join him on a walk in his garden and other more quiet and peaceful parts of his premises.

In the process of saying goodbye, sometimes he would invite a friend or associate to take a walk in the park together, and he realized that his first meeting with them would also be his last.

MOVE IT UP!

Most of us promise ourselves that one day we will slow down, spend more time with our family, spend a lazy day out with our friends, or maybe take a walk alone by the seashore. If you are like one of the many that think this way, O'Kelly has three words for you – Move It Up!

Last but not least, don't delay doing something until tomorrow when you can do so today because nobody knows what the future holds.

If you have decided that something is important for you, why not do it now, so you can have more time to enjoy the fruits of your labor for a longer duration?

Don't delude yourself that you'll always have more time to do it tomorrow, as it may never come.

Take for example, when people go for holidays and there are many places to go, sometimes they will tell themselves, "We missed out on this place, but never mind, we will come back next time," but it's more likely that they will never come back to the place again. It is probably the only time they would go to that place or that country.

So, treasure every moment that you still have and move it up, before it is too late.

If you have a goal, direction, and a dream to fulfill, move it up! Go forth and fulfill it while making a conscious effort to schedule time to savor nature and the environment, bond with your family and friends, and practice being in the moment.

Let us rather be 100 days early to plan our path, than 1 day too late.

So the moral of the story is that if you know what you want, and if it is meaningful and important to you, then don't wait. Do it now, before it is too late.

Don't take things for granted because time is fleeting, and you may not know when your number is up – then it would be too late.

So, in Eugene's case, by slowing down, he actually was able to focus better, not the next two months, not next week, or even the next few hours but in the next 60 seconds of his life.

From this story, if you want to enjoy a quality, meaningful and purposeful life, the most important thing to remember is that life is not about chasing something in the future; it is about being in the moment, fully conscious of your surroundings and the environment, and realizing how beautiful it can be.

That is the essence of Wealthy By Choice: being aware of the important things in life, and choosing those things first, whether it is a healthy lifestyle, enjoying fulfilling relationships, or achieving financial independence. Because once you have discovered your true life purpose, everything begins to fall in place and make sense in the end, and you will have more happiness, joy, fun, and love in your life!

The Path to Sustainable Wealth Action Steps

Life is about more than just quickly fattening up your bank account. Part III went deeper into the Wealth Mentors' holistic approach to wealth creation and management while focusing on quality of life. Complete the corresponding exercises found in the *Wealth Creation Workbook*. These exercises help you connect with your value and purpose and take action on what matters to you the most. Go now to www.wealthybychoicebook.com/bonus and download your free PDF copy of the *Wealth Creation Workbook*.

CONCLUSION

Congratulations, you've made it this far and I hope you have gained new insight on how to manifest wealth choices.

As this book comes to a close, I hope that what I have shared with you has given you enough insight to inspire an inevitable action in your life: to apply this knowledge that most working professionals or aspiring wealth creators simply never have access to. For me – even to share it with you, is in every sense of the word: a blessing.

Everything that has helped me accumulate wealth has been challenging on every level of my being. My beliefs, peers, and personal capability have all been stretched and put into question. But hanging in and staying the long course has really paid off. I hope that you too, choose to continue your journey with wealth forever.

ACTION BREEDS CLARITY

Everything contained in this book has a lot of wealth-building power; however, not everything you read in this book will be something you apply immediately. You are human after all. All I ask is that you embrace a part of it to start and revisit the text as you grow your wealth and yourself, as a person. Don't let it be just another book. Let it be a mentor that is for and with you, for as long as you live.

And no matter what results you achieve in life, I am certain you will continually find more layers to explore to deepen your experience of wealth. It may take a few months, a few years, or maybe for some, just a small few tweaks that only take days. Time doesn't matter. As long as you have started, you can get there. I remember being in Sydney, Australia, and looking at the waves hitting the face of the cliffs, and it dawned on me how consistent action from the waves has shaped the face of the cliff over many years. What seemed like just water splashing on an immovable wall of rock was in fact much more. It was a force that helped shape the very nature of that rock. So, too, are the daily actions you take towards building and sustaining wealth in your life actions that are proven to work.

So if you have given it your all to embrace as many principles as possible, you will no doubt be much clearer about the purpose you have in life and what you want of money to support that ideal version of your lifestyle because that ideal version, by definition, is wealth. Your wealth lake! If you have applied the principles from even just the first few chapters, by now, you will be clearer on why you want wealth to start with, for without that clarity, wealth will only stay as a possibility for your life rather than manifesting as a reality. Over time, you will continue to clarify what you want because we are human beings living in a dynamic environment and change is a natural part of life.

Along the way, you will have also discovered your natural strengths and talents to decide where you want to start building your wealth. Is it trading? Is it learning the delicate and timeless art of smarter selling? Or are you someone who would really love to craft a personal brand and impact lives by being yourself? That's the gift. Through introspection, we get clear on the outward expression that will best suit the versions of life we want to live. Remember, the vehicles for wealth are different by nature because they are best suited to people of differing natures.

Over the years, I have diversified the wealth engines I use. As such, I suggest you also get a good feel for all the wealth engines. Understanding the overarching principles to a competent degree will add dimension to your primary wealth creation vehicle – the one of your choice. It will also be obvious to you that wealth creation is much more than simply accumulating money.

You are now more than just armed with quality information about the different wealth engines available for you to build wealth; you are also equipped with what I believe are priceless and timeless strategies: the internal and personal development knowledge that you simply must have in order to be wired for success in the long run. You can be *Wealthy By Choice*.

WEALTH IS AN INSIDE JOB

You also have a frame and a process to follow for wealth creation. Not rigid, but supportive, just like the post that supports a growing baby tree. We have simply set the basic framework so that you can familiarize yourself with it and add to it step-by-step. Over the course of time, as your wealth builds and sustains, revisit the *Wealth Creation Workbook* and reconnect with the exercises. Let your responses grow and develop alongside your monetary growth. If you haven't yet, get your complimentary copy at www.wealthybychoicebook.com/bonus.

JUST AS GROWTH IS NATURE'S WAY, SO IS TRUE WEALTH

In the first chapter of this book, I shared with you the 6-steps you can take to create and sustain wealth in your life:

1. **Articulate** Why You Want Wealth, What You Want for Your Life, and How Much You Want.
2. **Understand** Where You Are Right Now In Terms of Your Financial Position.
3. **Get Clearer** on Your Values, Natural Strengths, and Skill Sets.
4. **Choose** the Best Wealth Engine to Start With.
5. **Accelerate** Wealth Creation by Executing the Right Strategies.
6. **Sustain** Your Wealth for the Long Run.

I hope they stick with you for the long run. As I continue my mission to empower the financial destinies of others, I am always keeping my hand on the pulse of the market – to incorporate more and more of the knowledge and training that can make a difference.

When I think back to how far Wealth Mentors have come in 10-years, I know for a fact there are many more exciting things on the horizon. And one of those things, I believe, is the frontier of human potential. A time where people will start to truly dig deep into how powerful their mind and spirit can be when we know how to work with it.

If there is one thread that connects all successful trainers and internationally renowned gurus I have seen, it's that they invest in developing themselves in all areas of life. They invest in nurturing their own human vessel to maximize performance. They go beyond their finances and live holistically. They choose eternal knowledge that stretches their boundaries and thus expands their life.

This is the sort of knowledge, or "life manual," that we never got when we were born into this world. As technology and science start to prove more and more of the amazing capabilities we have inherent in us to create the life we want, I believe we will start to see a fundamental shift from just tactical knowledge into the philosophy of building wealth both inside and out.

I hope this inspires you and gives you the confidence knowing that what you have learned in this book is putting you at the forefront of what is to come. That future is exciting beyond imagination!

In the pursuit of wealth, take personal responsibility in your life to not just focus on whatever is out there, but to enjoy what you already have. And do the right thing, for it will take you a long way indeed.

I hope that this poignant message will awaken you to cherish these hidden values in life that money cannot buy.

True Wealth is to cherish and protect your Health, the quality of your Relationships, and most of all the value of your Time because these are the things that matter most in the end.

Don't regret and realize it too late when the moment is gone. Do what you can, with what you have, wherever you are.

To Your Wealth, Success, and Happiness,

Aaron Sim

ACKNOWLEDGMENTS

Tracy Wong – To my dear wife Tracy, thank you for connecting me to my higher purpose and guiding me to the different instructors that have helped me build the foundations of my success. And of course, I couldn't do that without your ability to care for me during my journey too, and for being such an incredible mother to our daughter Cherie. I am so grateful for this loving relationship that is also a partnership – where our different gifts complement each other so well.

Cherie Sim –Thank you for giving me a new way of dealing with challenges in my life. You have a calm way of dealing with people, being diplomatic, and bringing people together for a cause. You have humbled me and shown me how to build rapport and trust, with my customers and my community. You are a blessing and you remind me that arguments are a product of differences and that communication resolves it because it brings you to a space of mutual understanding.

Mirriam MacWilliams – I really want to acknowledge you as my first trainer, who allowed me to build wealth and leave the corporate world. You were my first business partner, and without you, I wouldn't have been able to catalyze my wealth creation process. You have a great passion and positive energy such that the first word out of your mouth every morning is "it's a beautiful day and I have it all." And today, that's exactly how I feel.

Joel Bauer – Thank you, Joel, for being so dedicated to inspire and provide immeasurable value to our students. Your ability to give, and keep giving, is a philosophy to life and business that not only impacts lives but expands who we are as individuals. Because of your commitment to extracting and disseminating all your decades of experience, students are getting results on an unprecedented level as I've never seen before. Bottom line, your systems work!

Derek Gehl – I thank you for your ability to train and teach our students from the ground up with systems and tools that work. More importantly, you recognize the need to adapt and test new ideas in business, in a rapidly changing business environment. Because of your pioneering, students can rest assured that they are taught the latest tools and tactics for what works, and that is priceless.

Skip Archimedes – Thank you for your flexibility and your masterful approach to connecting feelings with logic and showing people how amazing the human body is, in its ability to heal itself. All of our students embrace your amazing ability to make the most out of unexpected situations, and more importantly, making them fun!

Wealth Mentors Students – Thank you for the opportunity to share my expertise; as I see you, I see myself in your shoes previously. It humbles me. I have realized that I grow more, as I help you grow too. My success is truly a product of the success I enable you to experience in life – they go hand in hand. I look forward to continuing to devote myself to help you do well both now and into the future, which looks amazing!

Jon Low – I thank you for guiding me through the process and sequence to extract this book from within. Without your secret knowledge and "know-how," I would have never finished it. It would have been but a thick pile of notes sitting on my bookshelf, with only the potential to impact lives. Today, with your help, it has materialized and is ready to be received by an audience who are hungry to build wealth in their lives today.

Jeffrey Slayter – Thank you for connecting me with Jon

Low, and your community of inspiring individuals who are committed to making a difference in their lives, and the lives of others. As a trainer, I am always touched by your incredibly heartfelt approach to causing transformation in people's lives and businesses. Keep pushing the fold!

Master Ching Hai – I acknowledge you for guiding me to do the right thing, in personally developing my spirituality. If I didn't know you, I would have continued down a pathway to self-destruction. Getting to know you has allowed me to guide myself beyond just my life. I am now able to create a legacy for future lives by serving my own purpose within this lifetime.

ABOUT THE AUTHOR

Aaron Sim is a #1 International Bestselling Author, global entrepreneur, business consultant, certified public accountant, wellness advocate, and CEO of Wealth Mentors. He has over thirty years of experience supporting the growth and performance of international corporations, entrepreneurs and businesses, international trainers, philanthropic ventures, and investment experts.

Aaron has been featured on Capital TV, PAS FM Radio, Sunday Times, Star, The Standard, and Shang Hai magazine. He has shared the stage with world-renowned speakers such as Joel Bauer, Armand Morin, and Alex Mandossian.

Aaron and his company Wealth Mentors, have served over 15,000 international clients throughout Singapore, Malaysia, USA, Hong Kong, Brunei, and Indonesia, educating them in his SIM Method (Simplify, Integrate, Monetize), which includes holistic living and sustainable wealth building to nourish all areas of their lives.

ABOUT WEALTH MENTORS

Wealth Mentors provides the world's most specialized and tailored trainings to enrich people's lives so they can experience more passion, purpose, fun, and freedom.

Since 2003, they have brought to Asia world-class trainers like Millionaire Trader Mirriam MacWilliams, Futures & Commodities Trader Larry Williams, Top Persuasion Guru Joel Bauer, and America's leading internet marketing and traffic expert Derek Gehl - all of whom provide wealth generation expertise that is not easily accessible in the south-east Asian region.

Aaron Sim invested hundreds of thousands of dollars traveling the world to discover the most specialized and customized training in trusted wealth vehicles to help people achieve real results with their finances, rather than temporary inspiration. That same approach is the foundation for what Wealth Mentors does today. The key is to explore the path to wealth that works best for you.

Find out more at www.WealthMentors.com.

NOTES

PREFACE

1. Contributors to Wikimedia projects. "Income Inequality in Malaysia." *Wikipedia,* 22 Jan. 2020, https://en.wikipedia.org/wiki/Income_inequality_in_-Malaysia.
2. "Number of Millionaires in Singapore to Surge 62% by 2025 to 437,000: Report." *The Straits Times,* 23 June 2021, https://www.straitstimes.-com/business/economy/number-of-millionaires-in-singapore-to-surge-62-by-2025-to-437000-report.
3. The Pew Charitable Trust. *Economic Mobility Across Generations: Pursuing the American Dream.*
4. *Bloomberg - How Did the World's Rich Get that Way?* https://www.bloomberg.-com/news/articles/2013-04-22/how-did-the-worlds-rich-get-that-way-luck.

1. WHAT IS WEALTH?

1. Jetley, Neerja. "Singapore's Multimillionaires: New Wealth Report Busts The Myths." *Forbes,* 27 Sept. 2013, https://www.forbes.com/sites/neerjajet-ley/2013/09/27/anatomy-of-a-singapore-multi-millionaire-a-new-wealth-report-busts-many-myths/?sh=36adab6e3b76.

5. YOUR WEALTH CONTROL CENTER

1. Ph.D., Bruce H. Lipton. *The Biology of Belief 10th Anniversary Edition.* Hay House, Inc, 2015.
2. Canfield, Jack. *Mastering the Art of Success.* Celebrity Press, 2017.
3. Ph.d., Shad Helmstetter. *The Power of Neuroplasticity.* CreateSpace, 2014.

7. SMARTER SELLING

1. McKinley, Mac. *Marketing Alignment: Breakthrough Strategies for Growth and Profitability.* Wheatmark, Inc. 2002.
2. Iverson, Jennifer. "Why Would Anyone Do Business with YOU?" *PASBA,* 28 Mar. 2019, https://www.pasba.org/why-would-anyone-do-business-with-

you/.
3. "Classics in the History of Psychology -- A. H. Maslow (1943) A Theory of Human Motivation." - *A. H. Maslow (1943) A Theory of Human Motivation,* http://psychclassics.yorku.ca/Maslow/motivation.htm.
4. Mcleod, Saul. "Maslow's Hierarchy of Needs." *Simply Psychology,* 29 Dec. 2020, https://www.simplypsychology.org/maslow.html.
5. McGregor, Douglas. *The Human Side of Enterprise.* 1966.

11. HEALTH IS WEALTH

1. Japsen, Bruce. "U.S. Workforce Illness Costs $576B Annually From Sick Days To Workers Compensation." *Forbes,* 12 Sept. 2012, https://www.-forbes.com/sites/brucejapsen/2012/09/12/u-s-workforce-illness-costs-576b-annually-from-sick-days-to-workers-compensation/?sh=17b414625db0.
2. Archimedes, Skip. *Living Forever Young: The 10 Secrets to Optimal Strength, Energy & Vitality.* Watkins Media Limited, 2018.
3. FACLM, Michael Greger, M. D., and Gene Stone. *How Not to Die: Discover the Foods Scientifically Proven to Prevent and Reverse Disease.* Flatiron Books, 2015.
4. "Average Night's Sleep Now Less than Six Hours, Survey Shows." *Safety+Health Magazine,* 4 Mar. 2020, https://www.safetyandhealthmagazine.-com/articles/19519-average-nights-sleep-now-less-than-six-hours-survey-shows.
5. NHS. "Why Lack of Sleep Is Bad for Your Health." *Nhs.Uk,* https://www.nhs.uk/live-well/sleep-and-tiredness/why-lack-of-sleep-is-bad-for-your-health/.

Made in the USA
Monee, IL
06 November 2026

68003069R00142